The Light Princess

a new musical

music and lyrics by
TORI AMOS

book and lyrics by
SAMUEL ADAMSON

suggested by a story by
George MacDonald

ff

faber and faber

First published in 2013
by Faber and Faber Limited
74–77 Great Russell Street
London WCIB 3DA

Typeset by Country Setting, Kingsdown, Kent CT14 8ES
Printed and bound by CPI Group (UK) Ltd, Croydon, CR0 4YY

© Samuel Adamson and Tori Amos, 2013

The right of Samuel Adamson and Tori Amos to be identified
as authors of this work has been asserted in accordance with
Section 77 of the Copyright, Designs and Patents Act 1988

All rights whatsoever in this work, amateur or professional,
are strictly reserved. Applications for permission for any use
whatsoever must be made in advance, before rehearsals begin,
to The Agency (London) Ltd, 24 Pottery Lane, Holland Park,
London W11 4LZ (kh-office@theagency.co.uk). No performance
may be given unless a licence has first been obtained.

*This book is sold subject to the condition that it shall not,
by way of trade or otherwise, be lent, resold, hired out
or otherwise circulated without the publisher's prior consent
in any form of binding or cover other than that in which
it is published and without a similar condition including
this condition being imposed on the subsequent purchaser*

A CIP record for this book
is available from the British Library

ISBN 978-0-571-30988-7

For Edward, Annie, Angus, Louis and Sophie
S.A.

*For all the light children
and teenagers everywhere*
T.A.

The Light Princess was first presented in the Lyttelton auditorium of the National Theatre, London, on 25 September 2013. The cast, in order of speaking, was as follows:

Voice of Six-Year-Old Althea Eve Elliott-Sidi
Voice of Eight-Year-Old Digby Connor Fitzgerald
Piper Amy Booth-Steel
Llewelyn Kane Oliver Parry
Althea Rosalie Craig
King Darius Clive Rowe
Digby Nick Hendrix
King Ignacio Hal Fowler
Zephyrus Ben Thompson
Serjeant-at-Arms Malinda Parris
Falconer Laura Pitt-Pulford
Mr Flowers David Langham
Mr Crabbe Adam Pearce
Mr Grey Caspar Phillipson
Lady Delphine Nicola Hart
Ensemble Vivien Carter, James Charlton,
    C. J. Johnson, Richard Lowe, Jamie Muscato,
    Landi Oshinowo, Phoebe Street
Acrobats Owain Gwynn, Tommy Luther,
    Emma Norin, Nuno Silva
Swings Stephanie Bron, Luke Johnson

Mari Yamamoto (*violin*), Joan Martinez (*violin*),
Douglas Harrison (*violin*), Leonie Adams (*cello*),
Elena Hull (*double bass*), Anna Stokes (*flute/alto flute*),
Nicola Hands (*oboe/cor anglais*), Sarah Thurlow
(*clarinet*), Lois Au (*bassoon*), Katherine Rockhill (*piano*),
Tom Brady (*keyboards*)

Director Marianne Elliott
Designer Rae Smith
Lighting Designer Paule Constable
Choreographer Steven Hoggett
Music Director and Supervisor Martin Lowe
Orchestrations John Philip Shenale
*Vocal Arrangements and Additional Orchestration*s
    Tori Amos and Martin Lowe
Animations Matthew Robins
Projection Designer Ian William Galloway
Puppetry Director Finn Caldwell
Puppetry Designer Toby Olié
Aerial Effects Designer Paul Rubin
Sound Designer Simon Baker
Associate Set Designer Paul Atkinson
Associate Choreographer Neil Bettles
Assistant Music Director Tom Brady
Staff Director Paul Foster
Producer for the National Theatre Tim Levy

Characters

Althea
the Light Princess of Lagobel, sixteen

Digby
the Solemn Prince of Sealand, eighteen

Piper
Althea's companion, an orphan, sixteen

Llewelyn
Prince of Sealand, Digby's brother, seventeen

King Darius
of Lagobel, Althea's father

King Ignacio
of Sealand, Digby and Llewelyn's father

Falconer
to the King of Sealand

Zephyrus
Digby's falcon

Serjeant-at-Arms
to the King of Lagobel

Mr Flowers
of Lagobel, Althea's suitor

Mr Crabbe
of Lagobel, Althea's suitor

Mr Grey
of Lagobel, Althea's suitor and betrothed

Lady Delphine
of Sealand, Digby's betrothed, sixteen

King's Physician
of Lagobel

Bishop
of Sealand

Servants, Guards, Courtiers, Soldiers, Lagobellans
of Lagobel

Soldiers, Courtiers, Sealanders
of Sealand

Musical Numbers

ACT ONE

Prologue: Once Upon a Time
*Piper, Llewelyn, Lagobellans, Six-Year-Old Althea (voice),
Sealanders, Eight-Year-Old Digby (voice), Althea*

My Own Land
*King Ignacio, Digby, Soldiers, Llewelyn, Sealanders, King
Darius, Althea, Servants, Piper, Falconer, Serjeant-at-Arms*

My Fairy-Story
Piper, Althea

Queen Material
Althea, King Darius, Piper, Guards, Lagobellans

Sealand Supremacy
Llewelyn, Soldiers, Falconer, Digby, Althea, Piper

Zephyrus Call, Levity? *and* Althea
Digby, Althea

Scandal
Serjeant-at-Arms, Lagobellans

The Gauntlet
King Darius, Lagobellans

Better Than Good
Althea, Servants

The Solution
*King Darius, Mr Flowers, Serjeant-at-Arms,
Lagobellan Courtiers/Servants, Mr Crabbe, Mr Grey*

Highness in the Sky *and* Proverbs
Digby, King Ignacio

Not a Fairy-Tale
King Darius, King Ignacio, Lagobellans, Piper

God, the Horror
Piper

No H2O
Althea, Piper

Zephyrus Call, Althea *reprise*,
Darkest Hour *and* Gravity
Digby, Althea

ACT TWO

Propaganda and Spin
Lagobellans, King Darius, Sealanders, King Ignacio

Amphibiava
Digby, Althea

Tinkle, Drizzle, Bubble and Gush
*Althea, Serjeant-at-Arms, Falconer, Digby, King Ignacio,
King Darius, Piper, Llewelyn*

Nothing More Than This
Digby, Althea

Queen of the Lake
Althea

Drought
Mr Flowers, Mr Crabbe, Lagobellans

The Whistleblower
Piper, King Darius, Serjeant-at-Arms, Lagobellans

My Little Girl's Smile
King Darius, Serjeant-at-Arms, Piper

Bitter Fate
Digby, Llewelyn

Zephyrus's Journey
Falconer

The Wedding
*Piper, Serjeant-at-Arms, Falconer, King Darius,
Sealanders, Llewelyn*

Crash in the Universe
*Digby, Althea, Llewelyn, Piper, Serjeant-at-Arms,
Lagobellans, Sealanders*

Tears *and* Gravity *reprise*
Althea, Digby

Epilogue:
Once Upon a Time *and* Coronation
*Piper, Llewelyn, Serjeant-at Arms, Falconer, Althea,
Digby, Company*

THE LIGHT PRINCESS

Note on Althea

Althea floats in the air.

To be on the ground, she must be 'weighted': by things in her hands – books, gold – or by people pulling ribbons attached to her dress, or holding her down. When the things are removed or let go, she rises. If she were outdoors and somebody didn't hold a ribbon or she didn't tie herself somewhere, she might rise for ever. On the whole, this detail isn't conveyed in dialogue or lyrics, and needs visual exposition. The stage directions don't usually indicate when, or how, she is grounded, nor when she is in the air and what's stopping her in that case from rising to the stratosphere.

In many scenes, humour should be extracted from her inability to do 'normal' things, or her ability to do them but in her unique fashion.

In Act One, her desire is to float, so whenever she's weighted it's out of necessity, or because someone wants to take her out of her comfort zone, or restrain her.

Act One

To fairy-tale music, Piper and Llewelyn bring a map to life. Three lands. Lagobel is yellow, arid, landlocked. Sealand is blue, lush, coastal. Between them is the inhospitable Wilderness, yellow meeting blue, therefore green.

Piper
Once upon a, once a –

Llewelyn
– once upon a time . . .

Piper
Lived a princess –

Llewelyn
– and a prince –

Piper *and* **Llewelyn**
– in kingdoms –

Piper
– gold –

Llewelyn
– and blue –

Piper *and* **Llewelyn**
– divided by a Wilderness of emerald.

Lagobel's royal family: King, Queen, fourteen-year-old Prince, four-year-old Princess.

Piper Lagobel was a scorching desert full of gold, ruled by a kind king and queen. The people adored them; but

3

one day, the Queen fell ill. Soon, she was dead, and shadows fell. The King wept, his son wept, everyone wept, so it seemed Lagobel, that had precious little water, was awash with sorrow.

Lagobellans
Though we have no H2O,
How our tears flow through our gold land,
Oh, the woe, the tears, the woe.

Piper Of all the people, only the little Princess's eyes stayed dry. To her, everyone's grief was a furious lagoon that wanted to drown her. So she tried to follow her mother to heaven by lifting her feet, and floating. From that day, Althea had no gravity, and never cried.

Lagobellans
The Light Princess of Lagobel.

Piper Because she was light, Althea couldn't ride or fight like her brother Prince Alexander, and refused to take anything seriously. The people wondered if she was a witch. Mortified by their hostility, her father King Darius felt compelled to lock her in the Tower with no friend except me, Piper, an orphan. With the Queen gone, the lame old King forgot the meaning of family and favoured only his son, the future King Alexander, who became a warrior, the people's champion. Althea was forgotten.

Six-Year-Old Althea
Far away from everyone's jeers,
High above their crocodile tears,
Locked away with Mother's old books;
Brother can shine,
I am just fine;
I do not cry
Here in the sky.

Sealand's royal family: King, Queen, two Princes. The music becomes anthemic.

Llewelyn To the east of Lagobel was its enemy, Sealand, a realm of bountiful coasts and mighty rivers ruled by the tyrant King Ignacio. One day, his wife questioned his tyranny, then mysteriously died. The people did not dare weep.

Sealanders
Even though the Queen is dead
There is no woe in our blue land.

Llewelyn But little Prince Digby did cry. As his mother went to heaven, his laughter followed her; and from that day, Digby's heart was so heavy, he never smiled.

Sealanders
The Solemn Prince of Sealand.

Llewelyn As Digby grew up he never put a foot wrong and his tyrant father saw in him nothing but a warrior to rival Lagobel's Alexander. Only the King's Falconer pitied the sad soldier, so one day she gave him his late mother's falcon.

The falcon, Zephyrus, is seen.

Eight-Year-Old Digby
Zephyrus soar
Zephyrus high,
Roar with the West Wind that bears your name . . .

Llewelyn The bird made Digby's life worth living. But neither Zephyrus, nor I, Llewelyn, his brother, could make him smile.

The music becomes majestic.

Piper Each kingdom craved the other's riches. The desert of Lagobel thirsted after Sealand's water.

Llewelyn Even with its bountiful coast, Sealand hungered for Lagobel's gold.

Piper Between them was a frontier known as the Wilderness. It was full of dangerous dragons and strange secrets, and kept the kingdoms separated.

Sealand drums.

Llewelyn Then, out of the blue, a Sealand spy shot Althea's brother Prince Alexander dead.

Drums out.

Piper In a second, Lagobel had no future king, and with its current king old and lame, its crumbling army and very future were in the hands of a floating Princess.

MY OWN LAND

The music throbs as Llewelyn joins his brother Digby, eighteen, who is seen at the Sealand palace with Falconer, Zephyrus and Soldiers. Enter King Ignacio, crown of sapphire.

King Ignacio
Son, it's time; seize the prize –
They're in chaos, you are ready,
You must mobilise!

Digby puts a scroll to Zephyrus's beak, then launches him: the bird flies off and away.

Digby
This is it, now soar, my friend;
Up into your realm of levity.
While I stay grounded here,
Underneath the thumb of gravity.
I submit to my fate; no choice;
This decisive moment was foretold.
Since Mother died I've trained
For the day the blue land seized the gold.

King Ignacio *and* **Sealanders**
Ev'rything is changing
Here on Sealand's shores –

King Ignacio
And you must kill the Light Princess.

Digby
The war to end all wars.

Llewelyn
Brother, Destiny is calling!

Digby
I will fight to expand
My own land –

Digby *and* **Sealanders**
My own land.

Focus the palace in Lagobel: in Althea's dingy room in the Tower, filled with books, Althea, sixteen, is floating in the air, Piper holding one of her ribbons. King Darius enters. He wears a crown of gold, uses a walking-stick, and is attended by his Physician. His spear-carrying Serjeant-at-Arms follows. He instructs a band of nasty Servants: they concoct nasty means to bring Althea down.

King Darius
Weight her down! It's absurd!
She is now the future Queen and
She is not a bird!

Althea
Not a bird, not a plane, a girl;
Just without a grain of gravity.
Below is gloom and woe;
Up above, a life of levity.

King Darius *and* **Servants**
    Ev'rything is changing
    Here in Lagobel.

King Darius
    Their crime means you're the Crown Princess –
Althea
    I won't go down to hell.
Piper
    Dear friend, Destiny is calling!

Althea
    No it's not! I can't stand
    My own land –

Althea *and* **Servants**
    My own land.

King Darius (*to Serjeant-at-Arms*) Make her wield a
spear. (*To Servants.*) Dust off her crown. (*To Althea.*)
Reassure the people: and with your feet on the ground.

Althea But, Father –

   But King Darius limps off. Servants prowl about
   Althea with a robe and golden symbols of royalty –
   crown, orb and spear – and, during the following,
   force them on to her. Piper is pushed aside.

Althea
    I float like a leaf in the sky,
    In a neverland immune to pain –

Servant
    Well now, bear some weight!

Piper (*to Servants*)
    Is that all for her?

Althea (*to Piper*)
    Are they insane? –

Things are looking very dim –

Althea *and* **Piper**
Like a scene from Brothers Grimm –

Althea
I've got déjà vu, I'm six-years-old
And where's my mother?

Servant 1 (*Woman*)
She can't ride a horse because she is light!

Servant 2 (*Man*)
She can't wield a spear, as if she can fight!

Servants 3 *and* **4** (*Women*)
The day the Queen died, the pangs and the pains!

Physician *and* **Servant 6** (*Men*)
But Althea laughed –
There's ice in her veins.

Women	**Men**
She won't make a queen	
Because she	
Is light!	Because
	She
Because she is light!	Is light, she is light!

*Althea is now robed, crowned and weighted with orb
and spear. Awkward, ungainly.*

Piper You look like Richard the Third.

Servants (*bowing insincerely*)
Althea Selma Isadora D'Arcy!

They prod her towards the people.

Servant 2 Get out there.

Digby marches towards the same in Sealand.

Althea	Digby
Ev'rything is / changing	Nothing Ever changes!
Here in Lagobel. Any second I will smash these Shackles into smithereens!	
	It's not in me to rebel.

Falconer
Digby, don't forget your mother . . .

Serjeant-at-Arms
God, we wish you were your brother!

King Ignacio is revealed. The Sealanders bow.

Sealanders
King Ignacio Dylan Constantine!

King Ignacio
Our majestic shores and rivers blue
Hold no candle to this prince!

King Darius is revealed. The Lagobellans bow.

Lagobellans
King Darius Phineas Montgomery D'Arcy!

King Darius
Deep beneath our thirsty desert,
Gold by the ton –
But it's worth nothing without my son.

Althea Father, what do I do?

King Darius Serjeant-at-Arms, give her the speech.

There is a speech for Althea; Digby's is extempore.
Awkwardness as Althea is unable to take the speech

because of the golden orb, etc., so it is held for her by the Serjeant-at-Arms. Althea does her best, but . . .

Althea

Lagobellan friends.

I know you weep for Alexander –

Melodramatic wailing.

I assure you, these hands have been trained to ride and fight all the way to Sealand's precious coast; I'm Cleopatra, Gloriana, Boudicca –

Boudicca, how ridiculous. I couldn't defend you miserable, hypocritical land-lovers even if I wanted to.

Digby

Sealand warriors –

Thanks to the bravest of you, Alexander is dead.

Cheers.

We've just heard his sister is out of her tower. The lame king thinks a flying girl will succeed him.

Heckling, laughter.

We'll cross the Wilderness, enter their desert, execute king and daughter and plunder their gold. Sealand evermore!

He raises his sword like Henry V. Tableau.

She wilfully throws down the unwieldy spear and orb.
Shock and tears from the Lagobellans. Free of some
weight and bent double, her crown and robe fall off.
She ascends into the air towards King Darius's balcony,
relieved, happy, lyrical.

I feel, I feel, I feel light!

As she reaches the balcony, the music segues to
Zephyrus's theme, and attention is drawn to him as he
flies on. He lands by Althea.

Althea Who are you, then? Aren't you the most beautiful
creature in the sky?

She takes the scroll from his beak and reads.

King Darius What is it?

Althea The Solemn Prince of Sealand declares war on us,
and he's coming to rip out your heart and mine. I think
I'll go back to the Tower now.

She leaves in her fashion. Chaos. In Sealand they
march towards the Wilderness.

Lagobellans
   Ev'rything is changing!

Sealanders
   Ev'rything is changing!

King Darius
   Ev'rything is changing
     now!

King Ignacio
   Ev'rything is changing
     now!

Lagobellans
   Ev'rything is changing!

Sealanders
   Ev'rything is changing!

King Darius
   No more light!
   She'll command!

King Ignacio *and* **Digby**
   He/I will fight
   To expand –

King Ignacio, Digby, Falconer *and* Llewelyn	King Darius *and* Lagobellans	King Ignacio, Digby, Falconer Llewelyn *and* Sealanders
My own land.	God help Lagobel!	
		Sealand Evermore!
	God help Lagobel!	
		Sealand Evermore!
	Help us	Sealand Now
	God Now, help us	Now, Sealand Now
	God Now!	Now!

MY FAIRY-STORY

Althea, floating, in her book-filled room in the Tower.
Piper.

Piper Well, Althea . . . that went well, didn't it?

Althea It wasn't my fault. I did manage to read that stupid speech.

Piper You also managed to float to the royal balcony.

Althea It's over now, we're home, we're safe.

Piper Till the Sealanders come and tear out your heart.

Althea Piper, forget it: all you have to do is pretend something never happened, then it didn't. We're fine; if the world's a mess, it's their problem. Now read one of Mother's books. *The Little Match Girl*, I think.

She giggles and floats contentedly as Piper searches for a book.

Piper Not again? I don't think there's a story in this room we haven't read a thousand times.

Althea You know, sometimes I feel sorry for you: that you're not as happy as I am.

Piper I'm happy you're happy, Althea.

The fairy-tale music. She settles and opens the book with a sigh.

Here in the Tower, where we belong. Well . . . another day, another fairy-story.

'Once upon a, once a, once upon a time,
Lived a match girl who would light
Her matches in
The dark,
And in the flames she'd see a seventh heaven . . .

. . . her mother had died, her father had left, the streets were hard and cruel. But with her matches and mind, she had a way to make her family flicker to life . . .'

She continues to read in pantomime as Althea's airborne world comes to fantastical life. Her mother and father are with her, floating.

Althea
In the air
Is a world of my dreams,
A story come true:
Father's here

14

And he's proud
I can ride,
I can fight.
Ev'ry night
I recite him a tale
Like Scheherazade . . .
He puts his hand in my mother's;
As they listen,
They kiss.
It's like this in my story:
My life's seventh heaven,
My mother's alive
And Father loves me,
My floating world, where I'm gravity-free!
All that I wish for's in
My fairy-story
Up high with my family.
Here Father loves me for who I am,
And he throws me a party
And he leads the games,
And I outshine all the other girls
By climbing the highest wall!
'I'm the Queen of the kingdom, ruler of you all!'
Then I race to the door at my father's call . . .

Suddenly her make-believe collapses and she is self-terrorised.

Oh, the woe, he is not there,
My mother's dead,
Is this a nightmare?
Does my father even love me?
If I'm to know I must go below –

She grabs something to weight her and heads towards the ground. She stops herself.

– Althea, stop!

Stay up there
Way down here
Is a dark abyss . . .

She rises and her floating world returns.

. . . Here's Mother's kiss . . .
Yes, it's bliss in my story:
My life's seventh heaven
My mother's alive
And father loves me,
My floating world, where I'm gravity-free!
All that I wish for's in
This fairy-story;
Why change the story?
My fairy-story
Up high with my family . . .

Piper '. . . and no one ever knew of the exquisite life the
Match Girl had dreamt for herself in the clouds. The End.'

QUEEN MATERIAL
*Enter the real Father, and Serjeant-at-Arms holding
Althea's crown, the declaration of war, the golden orb
and sceptre. Piper genuflects.*

Althea Oh . . . Father . . . hello.

King Darius What do you think I should do, Althea?

Althea I was a disaster, I know . . .

King Darius . . . Never mind Sealand, our own people
may kill us.

Althea Did you forget when I was six and I floundered at
everything you forced me to do –

King Darius You're sixteen now. By now your brother
had commanded the army and discovered ten gold mines.

Althea Father, could we go together to visit Mother's grave?

King Darius A declaration of war. They murdered my son. Our soldiers' spirits are crushed. And what do you do? You fly.

Althea Float, actually. You don't understand that I can't help the way I am –

King Darius I father you, you throw my love back in my face.

Althea Your *love*, Father? I'm sorry, I'm confused, because I can count the times you've visited me on one hand and it's twice today. I embarrassed you, you banished me. You may have been 'Father' to Alexander, but not to me.

King Darius They look to you for strength.

Althea Is he deaf?

King Darius Come down.

Althea No, this is me . . . now read, Piper . . . um, *Peter Pan* –

Music, belligerent.

King Darius You will change, Althea, you are the *Crown Princess / of Lagobel* –

Althea (*interrupting*)
    Yes, I know; yes, I know
    How you want me to be Queen
    'Cause my brother's quit the scene
    And you fear the guillotine –!

King Darius We'll lose Lagobel. Our survival depends on your ability / to command our soldiers –

Althea

Yes, I know: 'Destiny',
I'm afraid I don't agree;
I say damn the royal line,
The fam'ly business isn't mine!
To hell with the imperial,
I'm not Queen material,
At six you said I had no worth,
So now I'll never come to earth!

King Darius

You are the child
Of Lagobel's King,
And the King's eldest child
Leads the army to glory;
Our charter dictates it,
The people expect it:
The royal child's the general –

Althea

Yes, you said, blahdy-blah
On and on and on you drone
How you need me on the throne –
I'm afraid the birdie's flown!

King Darius

I was the child
Of Lagobel's King,
Don't assume I don't know
Of the weight of this mantle;
My father, he forced it,
So don't make me force it.
I'm lame, I'm old and I'm dying –
Just acquiesce,
Just say yes, be their general –

Althea

Yes, I heard: it's my 'Fate',
But, you see, I don't relate:

You disowned me long ago,
They call this reaping what you sow!
To hell with the imperial –

King Darius Enough –

Althea
I'm not Queen material,
At six I was no use to you
So shove your crown up your wazoo!

That's pushing it, and the music turns magisterially.

King Darius
Dare you laugh to-
Day? You'll find your
Gravity of
Mind, by God, girl,
You must fight the
Foe with weapons
On the ground where
Kings have trod; girl,
Demonstrate some
Majesty, your
Army needs you
To be normal!
Father screamed the
Same at me, don't
Make me be King Lear.
It's war – now wield a spear!

He pulls her down and makes her take spear, orb and crown. They weight her.

Heed me, Princess:
Wear this crown,
I swear to God you will stay down,
My girl, you're cut *(re: himself)* from mighty cloth,
Therefore you're Queen material!

Your army is mobilising. Galvanise them, and lead them
to Sealand.

He leaves with the Serjeant-at-Arms.

Althea
The audacity, God, I hate him,
We are running away –

Piper
We are?

Althea
We are,

She flails at the bookcase.

Now find my mother's map,
Her compass, Alexander's car.

Piper
Did you say Alexander's car?

Althea
I did.
Drive me away to the West!

Piper
But that's the desert, there's no H_2O! –

Althea
Then damn it, we'll go to the East!

Piper
The Wilderness? Where there are dragons? –

Althea
No!
They're myths! The only
Dragon to fear is Father
It's from *him* that I must flee,
And it's there I'll find a sanctuary.

Piper But what about the war, there'll be fighting there.

Althea No worse than here. We'll go off the beaten path, right into the mountains.

I will live a life of light
In the forest like Snow White,
Free
From monarchical hostility!

She is about to rid herself of the crown, etc., but Piper stops her.

Piper Wait: if you mean this, Althea, *that's* what will get us past the palace guards. All right, we'll do it. But till we're out, keep your crown on and do as I say.

She helps the weighted Althea to walk-float out of the room, and they are in a corridor, but a weapon-wielding Guard is in their faces.

Guard (*whistling and calling for help*) Fugitive princess!

Piper You. We want to go beyond the gates to visit her mother's grave and command you give us the keys. (*To Althea.*) Say it, be who they want you to be.

Guard Back in the Tower!

Piper
Oh, go to hell, she is your future Queen!

Althea
I'm not!

Piper
You are!
And he is just a peasant!
'Obey me, sir,' just order him, he's dirt!

And as the Guard capitulates, they are with a line of Guards, all the way to the Palace gates.

Althea

Obey me, or I'll throw you in the dungeon!

The Guard unlocks a door. Another Guard. Althea's confidence builds.

Defy me and your family will starve!

The Guard unbolts a door. Another Guard, who also obeys. Etc.

The key!

Guards

The woe!
How we miss Alexander!

Althea

Obey! Or you'll be shorter by your head!

Guards

You mean to say –?

Althea

You'll be decapitated!
My brother's dead so I'm the guv'nor –

Althea *and* **Piper**

Turn the bloody key, and . . .

They are out of the Palace.

Oh, my God, we're free! And . . .

Althea rids herself of crown, spear and orb, though Piper manages to rescue the spear.

Althea

. . . I'm done, Father,
Keep your crown!
I swear you'll never bring me down!
This bird will out-fly all of you –
I am not Queen material!

The Palace disappears and they are in a car. Piper is at the wheel; she has a map.

Piper
Don't think for a single moment that I can drive this.
No, don't laugh, Althea, I mean it, we won't survive
this.

*They travel through Lagobel towards the Wilderness.
The music becomes mournful. A gold-coloured
battalion of Lagobellans is seen marching
disconsolately to the war.*

Althea Is that our army?

Piper Yes. Heading to Sealand.

Althea Heading to ruin, by the looks of it. They look so
despondent.

Is that normal?

Piper
Don't ask me . . .

Lagobellan Army
Oh, the woe, we're about to be thrashed;
Since the Prince died our world has crashed.
Lagobel is doomed – we are doomed –
The dark reign of the Light Queen . . .

Althea I see.

Piper What?

Althea They've given up. Because of me. The poor things.

Goodbye, kingdom:
Keep your crown,
Although you'll never bring me down,
I see the fear inside your souls . . .

Piper
The stuff of Queen material?

Althea No: of a wise, worldly woman.

Piper Naturally. Huh, the Serjeant-at-Arms!

The spear-wielding Serjeant-at-Arms, in Lagobellan gold, is part of the battalion.

Serjeant-at-Arms Your Highness? You came?! Just when we need you – you're like your brother after all! –

Althea (*to Piper*) No, she scares me, I'm nothing like my brother, head for the hills!

Piper The map, the maaaaaaaaaaaaap!

They take a sharp corner, veer from the path, and the map is lost to the wind. The music turns eerie. Eyes of wild creatures are seen in the trees.

Althea We're lost, aren't we?

Piper Utterly.

Althea Perhaps veering from the path wasn't such a smart idea.

Piper Oh, what makes you say that?

A dragon flies out of nowhere and attacks them. Piper screams. With more luck than design, Althea manages to swipe its head off with her spear. A geyser of crimson blood from the dragon's neck.

Althea
What just happened?

Piper
Don't ask me . . .

Althea
Take that, Father:

Keep your crown!
I swear you'll never bring me down!
I've strength to smite a dragon dead –

Piper
I'm thinking Queen material?

Althea Rubbish, I'm just a naturally gifted warrior.

Piper Yes, of course. We're the only people to have been this far into the middle of nowhere. Oh my God, we're never going to find our way out.

Althea Piper, look!

Piper Is it the sea?

They have chanced upon a beautiful lake, an oasis in the wilds. Swans duck, lilies flower, frogs leap. The music shimmers, the light glimmers. Althea and Piper are astounded.

Althea
No, it is a lake, a hidden lake,
Way off the beaten track. I am a desert girl,
Yet I know this is something rare, look at it gleaming,
A secret deep within the Wilderness, I'm dreaming –
Am I dreaming?

Piper
Don't ask me . . .

Althea Give me the compass! Look, there's an outlet, and water flows *west*. And *east* is an inlet, see, so the lake's probably filled from the Sealand coast. This could be the spring for everything; how Lagobel drinks.

Bad luck, Father:
Keep your crown!
I swear you'll never bring me down.
I've found the lake that gives us life . . .

25

They see a bird. It is Zephyrus the falcon, who makes beautiful patterns in the air.

I know that beautiful bird. He's my friend from Sealand.

Piper
You've learned of fear in people's souls –

Althea
In people's souls!

Piper
You've strength to smite a dragon dead –

Althea
A dragon dead!

Piper
You've found the lake that gives us life –

Althea
Gives us life!

Piper
By God, you're Queen –

Althea
I am not Queen! Perhaps I'm Queen? Could I be Queen?

Piper
By God, you're Queen –

Althea *and* **Piper**
– material!

SEALAND SUPREMACY

They disappear as military drums pound beneath a burst of the Sealand anthem. The moon comes out, and we are in a clearing in the Wilderness at the climax of a ferocious battle between the blue Sealand army, which includes the Falconer, and the golden Lagobellan one. Digby kills the last Lagobellan. He is bloody and muddy. At first, standing atop a pile of slain Lagobellans, Llewelyn gives voice to victory, goading Digby to celebrate. Zephyrus flies on.

Llewelyn
The golden army dead!
It's as my brother said:
That Alexander would turn in his tomb!
And this is just the start,
Next up, his sister's heart,
The witch impaled on the end of her broom!
They are defenceless now!
(*To Digby.*) So why the furrowed brow?
Just smile; for once, Digby, banish your gloom!
Sealand supremacy –

Sealand Soldiers
Sealand supremacy!
Sealand supremacy!
Supremacy!

Falconer
What you have done
Has brightened the world,
I can feel it; just
What you have won –
Who knows? But
Something is glimmering somewhere.

Llewelyn
Here!

Falconer
Who knows? but –

Llewelyn *and* **Falconer**
Something is glimmering –

Llewelyn
Falc'ner, it's –

Llewelyn *and* **Falconer**
Glimmering –

Llewelyn
Here!

Sealand Soldiers
All hail the solemn one!
You are your father's son
So feel the ecstasy
Of conquest, of glory,
Of our superiority,
Su-supremacy
Super-super-super-super-super-su-supremacy!
What is, what is theirs
Is now, is now, is now ours:
What stands between their gold and us?!

Althea and Piper are seen hidden in the trees.

Sealand Soldiers
What is, what is theirs
Is now, is now, is now ours:
what stands between their gold and us?!

Althea Look what they've done. Those are our soldiers,
the ones we saw.

Piper That's the Solemn Prince, isn't it?

Althea Defenders of my mother's kingdom. And Sealand's
swaggering over them. I can't bear it, I can't look.

Digby
What is, what is theirs –

Althea
Wha-at do I, do I do?

Digby *and* **Sealand Soldiers**
What stands between their gold and us!

28

Digby

What is, what is theirs –
Is now, is now, is now
   ours!

Althea

Wha-at do I, do I do?

Althea

What stands between? –

Piper

Just you!

Althea

Not me!

Sealand Soldiers

Sealand supremacy!
Sealand supremacy –

Falconer

What you have done has

Sealand supremacy!
Sealand supremacy!
Sealand supremacy!
Supremacy!
Sealand supremacy!
You feel the ecstasy?
Sealand supremacy!
Supremacy!
Sealand supremacy!
Sealand supremacy!
Sealand supremacy!
Supremacy!
Supremacy!
Sealand supremacy!
Sealand supremacy!
You feel the ecstasy

Brightened the
World, I can feel it; just
What you have
Won –
Who knows? But
Something is glimmering
Somewhere,
Something is glimmering
Somewhere,
Something is glimmering,
Digby, it's shimmering,
Somewhere,
Digby, it's glimmering,
Somewhere.

Althea

I can't look I
Can't look –

Of conquest, of glory,
Of our superiority
Su-supremacy

29

Super-	Let's
Super-	
Super-	Go
Super-	
Super-	Let's
Su-su-	
Supremacy!	Go!

Music pauses as in her panic, Althea reveals herself.
Althea I, I, I'm Althea D'Arcy, daughter of the late
Queen of Lagobel, and my brother was killed in your
name, and, and I don't have a sword –

Soldiers circle. Piper is restrained. Digby is astounded.
Llewelyn laughs.

Digby It's not possible . . . We're drunk.

Llewelyn Except there she is . . . the holy grail, flying.
Laugh, Digby –

Music resumes as he and Soldiers tug at the ribbons.
Digby aims his gun at Althea.

– if ever there was something to laugh at, here at last it is.

Digby
  There within my sight, the Light Princess –
  Oh, what a twist of fortune
  Underneath a Sealand moon!

ZEPHYRUS CALL *and* LEVITY?

As Digby shoots, Zephyrus swoops first on the gun, then
to Althea's rescue, grabbing her ribbons in his beak and
flying off with her to a syncopated version of his music.
Piper screams 'Althea!' In the mêlée Piper finds a means
of escape: chase music. The Falconer and Soldiers pursue
the bird, and Piper, into the Wilderness, but they lose
bird, girl, and each other. The music returns to the

Zephyrus theme; time passes as Digby traverses the Wilderness.

Digby
Zephyrus I
Zephyrus, call,
Roar with the West Wind that bears your name;
My only friend
You are my all,
How could you leave?
Answer my call.

ALTHEA

Digby finds himself at the lake. The music shimmers.

Digby Where am I?

And is that a lake? A hidden lake?
Way off the beaten path. I am a naval man,
Yet I know it's beyond compare, look at it shimmer,
Is this the thing the Falc'ner meant, is this the glimmer?

Zephyrus flies on with Althea as the lake music finishes. Her eyes are still closed; she frenziedly mutters her childhood song, a cappella.

Althea
Royal Princess, follow the Queen,
High above this sinister scene . . .

Digby takes her ribbons. He circles, amazed. She dares to look.

Oh. You. You shot at me and I'm unarmed. Bird, take me away from him; bird, please.

Digby Look at you. It's true. Yet you're nothing like they say . . .

Music ripples, suggesting the Prologue.

. . . How . . . how –

How can it be that you're flying?

Althea I don't fly, I float. What are you going to do to me? Let go.

Digby So you float. You're in the air . . . Perpendicular or . . .

He pulls at her ribbons, manipulating her.

. . . horizontal . . .

Althea Stop . . .

Digby . . . or – woah – rotational.

Althea (*upside down*) Yes, I'm very versatile –

Digby
How does it feel to be floating?

Althea Feel? It feels . . . please don't hurt me. Bird, help me.

Digby It's incredible, you don't have wings . . . and aside from *this* –

He moves her.

– you're almost normal.

Althea Let me go or, or, or I'll kill you, I will.

Digby Kill me? You can't even walk.

> So the physics:
> If I drop this ribbon
> You would keep ascending
> Till you met your ending?
> You'd be toast.
> Seems to me

Floating's not
Very versatile.

He puts his hands to his mouth to stop an unstoppable reflex: to smile, or even laugh.

Althea What, what, what, I don't understand anything you're doing or saying!

Digby
I don't either:
You're my mortal foe, but
Seeing you so useless –
What I mean is hopeless –
Makes me want . . .
Makes me want –

Althea
Spit it out.

Digby
Makes me want to smile –
Levity? It can't be –

'Levity' is self-reflective, and during it Zephyrus sees his chance, grabs the ribbon and flies off with Althea. Digby pursues them as the music darkens . . .

Zephyrus! Zephyrus! . . .

Althea Zephyrus? Like the West Wind, what a beautiful name.

The music soars then fades as Digby takes in his surroundings again.

Digby Is that water flowing out of the lake going west?

Althea It goes no distance.

Digby As far as Lagobel?

Althea Now you must give me a sword, because I'm neither useless nor hopeless, and history won't smile on you for flouting the rules of combat.

Zephyrus squawks at Digby. Althea tries to attack Digby.

Digby He's telling me that you're lovely.

Serjeant-at-Arms emerges from shadows, spear aimed at Digby. They don't see her.

Althea Only one of us leaves here alive.

She manages with a ribbon to strangle him, and they become locked in battle. She holds her own, it is fierce, and the Serjeant-at-Arms, impressed, drops her sword.

Digby Stop it, I don't want to hurt you! You don't have to fight, Althea, you don't have to prove anything!

A chord.

Althea You won't go back to your father with knowledge of this lake.

Digby
        Pretend within your hand
        You're holding a glass made out of crystal –

Althea I'll smash your face with it –

Digby
        Then with this hand try and reach
        For those apple blossoms that are fragile.

Althea With this hand, I'll break your neck –

Digby
        Just arch your back,
        Sweep the night away –

34

Althea

Who do you think, let me go, do you think you are?
Now
Give me a knife and I will slay you like a dog,
Let me go,
Do you think I am your
Prey? Some
Weak, exotic bird?

Digby

No! – no, you are Althea . . .

And with the golden ribbons tumbling and criss-crossing, glorious, balletic human patterns are created in the night sky. Zephyrus soars and circles.

You are, you are Althea –
You are changing the world for me,
You are heaven-sent –
A vision of golden light falling!
Just look at me,
Look into my eyes –

Althea

But, sir –

– there's procedure in a war.

Digby Did you go to school, or did you have a governess?

Althea What? Incredible that I'm above you yet you can still talk down to me.

Digby You're adorable.

Althea You're meant to be solemn.

Digby I know.

Althea So why are we dancing?

Digby No idea, I never have.

Althea Nor have I, stop it, fight!

Digby
> Open your frame, that's it –
> Now roll your lovely neck – just a touch –
> Lay your body back to the music,
> Gently swing those hips.

Althea
> This is confused, I could kill, it is so confusing,
> I want to tear you into strips, you are a dull,
> Self-obsessed
> Casanova. But those
> Lips. I'm
> Not a floating freak.

Digby
> No! – No, you are Althea . . .
> You are, you are Althea –
> You are changing the world for me,
> You are heaven-sent –
> A vision of golden light falling . . .
> Light falling.
> Look down –

Althea
> I just don't know what to say to you –

Digby
> Just look at me!
> Look into my eyes –

Althea
> But, sir –?

Digby
> I will never, no never do you harm –

Althea
> Never do me harm?

Digby
I will never, no never do you harm.

Entwined in ribbons, they kiss. Serjeant-at-Arms reveals herself.

Serjeant-at-Arms Mother of God.

Enter Falconer, with Piper her captive at the point of a blade.

Falconer Mother of God.

Serjeant-at-Arms (*re: Digby*) You're dead.

Falconer (*to Serjeant-at-Arms, re: Piper*) Move and she is.

Althea Drop your spear, Serjeant-at-Arms –

Digby Falconer, let her go –

Althea *and* **Digby** (*together*) I command it as your future Queen / King!

Piper Althea, what do we do, his soldiers will kill us!

Digby Go.

Falconer But, Your Highness. Your father, you know your duty –

Digby My duty, to kill them? The three of you, get out of here. Go!

Music grooves as Piper pulls Althea away.

Falconer, never tell a soul about that lake!

SCANDAL
Lagobel, where the Serjeant-at-Arms tells her story to the mob.

Serjeant-at-Arms Lagobellans, our army was massacred!

37

Lagobellans No!

Serjeant-at-Arms Wait, there's more! I was searching for
  survivors when I heard a familiar voice:

> It was *her*,
> She was there –
> You-know-who
> In the air –

Gasps; mouths open; they begin to question her.

> Let me speak!
> It's a corker:
> She'd captured the foe!
> Undeterred
> By her flaws
> She had him
> In her claws,
> And I thought,
> 'What a hero,
> We've misjudged her so!'
> And then came the blow:
> She snogged him –!

Lagobellans
  – God, no!

*Having scandalised the mob, Serjeant-at-Arms makes
her way to King Darius.*

Lagobellans	Serjeant-at-Arms
Oh, my God!	He
An affront!	Was
She was there!	Hers
What a stunt!	To
Couldn't fight!	Slay!
Couldn't save us,	

The mis'ry, the woe!
And there's one
Final cut
She is light
And a slut!
With the *Prince*!
She's a traitor!
He's her Romeo!
What a stain –
Dirty deed –
Does it mean –?
Foreign seed –!
What a blight!
Interbreeding!
How low can she go!
Has a fling
And it's us
In the muck!
What a huss!
And the King?
What does *he* think?
We all want to know!

Lagobellan 1
Had
Her
Dir-
Ty
Way!

Lagobellan 2
Could
Have
Killed
The
Foe!

Serjeant-at-Arms
And
The
King
Must
Know!

The music continues grooving as the protesting
Lagobellans gather beneath King Darius's balcony;
King Darius is seen above with Serjeant-at-Arms.

King Darius And as well as debauchery, she saw our army but refused to rally them?

Serjeant-at-Arms (*nods*) Every one of those soldiers was slain.

King Darius They'll hang me for this . . . what am I going to say?

39

Lagobellans

Our army is dead!	**Serjeant-at-Arms**
And it's all her fault!	(*to King Darius*)
This will make you wince:	That's what
Jig-jig with the prince!	Comes of
He was in her claws!	Light!
And now we're in his	
What will the King do?!	
Her mother would weep!	Her mother would weep!

THE GAUNTLET

King Darius on his balcony; Serjeant-at-Arms with him.

King Darius My people, the morning after our terrible defeat and it's not Sealand storming my palace, but you, as if your gripes about my daughter are a bigger challenge than those eastern savages. They are not.

I am not bowed by the crowd's dissent:	
It is *you* who is challenged!	
One of you must know of a remedy,	
Where's the man who can	
Cure her of light?	
He'll marry her.	
Get water, too:	
Half my	**Lagobellans**
Stores –	Free H2O?
You heard me right.	Did we hear right?

Lagobellans freeze as lights pick out King Darius and Serjeant-at-Arms:

Serjeant-at-Arms Marry her, sire?

King Darius I'm at a loss. I need an heir I can trust; I won't die without one. And I'll take him from her. Yes, that's it . . . I'll train him. She'll come down, marry, bear the child; and behind doors, I'll make him a King, and ensure the D'Arcy future.

The peril is near
Because she's afloat!

Lagobellans
Because she is light
That thug's at our throat!

She burns us with shame
Because she's afloat!

She burns us with shame
Because she's afloat!
Perhaps it is time
That we had the vote?!

I won't get an heir,

King Darius	**Women**	**Men**
We've not got	We've not got	
A prayer –	A prayer –	If she re-
If she re-	If she re-	Mains light, if
Mains light!	Mains light!	She's light!

King Darius (*back to the people*)
There is my gauntlet:
Bow, I am King!

The people obey, but whisper mutinously:

Lagobellans
What man would marry that . . .
Heartless floating spawn of the devil?

BETTER THAN GOOD

Althea's room, where the gang of nasty Servants is nastily burning/ripping up all the books, and nastily dressing Althea. Piper tries to stop them, but is pushed away. Althea floats, ducking and diving, euphoric.

Servants
Sealand bombarded our army with bullets
But Darius wants us to dress the Princess.
Her – a princess? What a charade:
Royalty's only about the façade.

Althea

The morning a-after the, the night before!
The story –

Servants

Scandalous!

Althea

Quite frankly I couldn't care less,
I'm the most disgraceful Princess!
Sweet bliss!
Care to hear more?

Servants (*variously*)

What were you thinking?
How did it happen?
They say you danced!

Althea

– Yes, an air ballet!

Servants

Devil's work, you are possessed!

Althea

Oh, I'm possessed! – shock! – how amazing!
For the first time in my life
I feel great – no, wait!
I feel one magnificent ache,
For the first time in my life
It feels good, better than good,
To be me!

Servants

What a rotten stunt,
What a rotten slight,
What an evil witch,
What a horrid plight,
Throw her mother's books
In the bloody fire!

Throw the orphan out!
Throw the orphan out!

Piper is thrown out, yelling Althea's name.

Althea
The morning after the, the night before,
The glory! The fury!

Servants
There are laws, there are taboos!

Althea
Well, I broke them and here is the news:
Finally, I am truly beginning to *feel.*
I seem to feel liking
For swooning and sighing –
(*Points to her lips.*) These seem to like smooching!
Sound all the trumpets, a prince
Dropped certain hints that he likes light girls!
For the first time I can feel
My legs ache – no, I must say:
My legs *quake*! And I must say:
He was one edible, delectable,
Muscular cake!
For the first time in my life
It feels good, better than good,
Better than I ever knew that it could –
For the first time in my life
It feels good, better than good,
To be me!

THE SOLUTION

Enter King Darius.

Darius Althea?

Althea Father –

Darius (*to Servants*) I told you to dress her.

Althea – I know I've caused a stink, but I want to tell you something: the Solemn Prince is all right, really, we should just all sit down and have a chat –

Serjeant-at-Arms rushes in, followed by Courtiers.

Serjeant-at-Arms Sire, a candidate!

King Darius Really? Show him in.

A chord. Mr Flowers is brought in. He is long-hàired, greasy, with a smoking opium pipe, a fairy-tale hippie. He presents his papers to King Darius.

King Darius
Name?

Mr Flowers
Zachary Flowers: thoroughbred Lagobellan.
And I have a cure, sir.

(*Re: reaching Althea; to Servants.*) I need a stairway to heaven.

King Darius
Premature, sir,
I want your diagnosis first!

Mr Flowers Addiction. High as a kite, King. Somewhere in here she's harvesting very magical mushrooms.

Althea I wish.

Mr Flowers So what she needs to come down: is a downer.

King Darius Is it safe?

Mr Flowers I use it every day.

Germanic vamp.

Althea Father – wait – that's not for me –?

44

Mr Flowers makes Althea inhale the opium pipe.

Mr Flowers
Poppy seeds with sage and thyme,
Don't resist, inhale the fumes.
There, there, baby, no big crime:
You ate too many magic shrooms.
Heartbeat slows –

King Darius
I'm uneasy –

Mr Flowers
Vision blurs –

King Darius
He's so sleazy –

Mr Flowers
Speech sluuuurrrrs!
Eyelids heavy, body queasy,
Drowsy, dozy, fuzzy-wuzzy,
Down –

King Darius
Down?

Serjeant-at-Arms
Down –

All
Down . . .!

Althea appears to have weight.

King Darius
You've done it, man!

But then Althea giggles. She rises, laughing her head off: she is tripping.

Why is she floating?

Courtiers/Servants
Floating, floating, floating like a
Wafting ginger freak with a ginger beak.

King Darius You're nothing but an opium fiend! Take him away!

Mr Flowers is carted off.

Mr Flowers She must be taking something very speedy – supplied by her Sealand chums, *Judas*.

King Darius Hopeless! – What options are left?

Serjeant-at-Arms There is a second, sire.

King Darius There *is*?

Mr Crabbe is brought in and gives his papers to King Darius. He is very fat, sweaty and sluggish. A more ghastly prospect than Mr Flowers.

Name?

Mr Crabbe
Octavius Crabbe: thoroughbred Lagobellan –

Althea (*stoned, interrupting*) Father, here's the major thing? In the Wilderness, I saw this, like, secret lake, it was uh-mazing, and I think it's the source for our tiny bit of H_2O?

I've found the lake that gives us life!

So we must, like, make sure the evil Sealand King doesn't control it, or with our droughts, we'd be, like, totally thirsty? Who's the roly-poly person?

Mr Crabbe
I have a cure. I can fix her.

(*To Servants.*) I need her close to me.

King Darius
How dare you?
Give me your diagnosis first!

Mr Crabbe Anorexia. All she needs is fattening up.

King Darius Well, that sounds harmless . . .

Vamp. A Courtier wheels on mountains of food.

Althea Father, no. I tried to do the right thing when I met the Sealanders, / truly –

She is shut up when she is force-fed.

Mr Crabbe
Crème brûlée and lard and bread,
Doughnuts, pasta, syllabub.
Girls like you are underfed,
They need some *fat*, now *eat your grub*!
Tummy bloats –

King Darius
I'm uneasy –

Mr Crabbe
Breathing slows –

King Darius
So uneasy –

Mr Crabbe
Gout grrrroooows!
Eyelids heavy, body queasy,
Glutted, sated, chocka-blocka,
Down –

King Darius
Down?

Serjeant-at-Arms
Down –

All
Down . . .!

Althea appears to have weight.

King Darius
You've done it, sir!

But then Althea convulses. The inevitable: she vomits the food. She rises.

Mr Crabbe (*protesting during the following*) No, no, no, all she needs is more cream puffs –

King Darius
Why is she floating?

Courtiers/Servants
Floating, floating, floating like a
Mutant bird-girl glitch; she's a puking witch.

King Darius Take him to the stocks! –

Mr Crabbe Then it's true, she's possessed by the Sealand Devil. The woe, the woe!

He is carted off. King Darius is losing self-control; Althea is traumatised.

Serjeant-at-Arms There's one more, a Mr Grey, he can't speak, a stammerer.

Althea Father, please –

King Darius Parents must make decisions for their children, *or children could just do the right thing.*

He turns straight to the stammering Mr Grey, now in the room, his papers held out.

Grey?

Mr Grey Y-y-y-y –

King Darius
Come to the point, sir!
I just need your cure, sir!

Mr Grey Y-y-y-your u-u-understanding; y-y-your love.

King Darius Love? I love her. But there's a royal
imperative –

Althea I should listen to Mother.

All eyes to her. She has recovered a little.

In the air she says, 'What a despicable man your father's
become.' I know what you want: you'll *never* get it. Why
would I bring a child into your world? We'd be better off
ruled by the evil Sealand King. I hope they *do* plunder all
our gold. Lagobel's over and it's your fault. I am the last
of the D'Arcys.

King Darius
My girl, you've gone too far,
Who do you think you are?
I have my own solution – I'll cure you, Althea.

Vamp returns.

Mr Grey: divorced, fertile, unable to speak. Son-in-law.
Bring them both to the dungeon.

Serjeant-at-Arms
Did he say the dungeon?

Courtiers/Servants
The dungeon.
He has his own solution,
He has his own so –

HIGHNESS IN THE SKY *and* PROVERBS
Althea disappears with a blood-curdling scream.
Romantic music. In Sealand, Digby is flying Zephyrus.

Digby

> Soar! Soar!
> Roar with the West Wind
> That bears your name.
> Soar, if I could
> I would like you do, like you do.
> Soar, venturer,
> If I could I would like you do.
> King of the falcons,
> You make my soul stir –
> But I've fallen for Her Highness in the sky,
> Highness in the sky,
> I have fallen!
> And you, you are not her . . .

> *Every single bird in the kingdom now appears, and in*
> *flocks they make sky-patterns as the starlings do.*
> *Enter Falconer then Llewelyn during the following;*
> *Falconer wrangles Zephyrus.*

> Soar! Soar!
> The sky is the limit,
> Skim the sun's flame.
> Monarchs of heaven
> You make my soul stir! –
> But I've fallen for Her Highness in the sky,
> Highness in the sky,
> I have fallen!

Falconer Your Highness, it makes me happy to see you like this, but your father –

Llewelyn Digby . . . we should have killed her straight away, pushed into Lagobel the second we defeated them. What's happened to you, why are you smiling?

Digby

> Ev'rything's changing,
> We're not as we were . . .
> For I'm soaring with Her Highness in the sky –

Llewelyn Digby –

Digby
> Highness in the sky,
> I am soaring!

Llewelyn But Father will kill us – what about me?

Digby
> And you, you are not her
> You are not her,
> Not her, not her . . .

> *Enter King Ignacio, with entourage: dogs, Soldiers.*
> *Zephyrus flies into the King's face, squawking; he*
> *shoos the bird away. The Falconer whistles.*

He's unafraid to show he doesn't like you, Father. 'A bird
may look at a King,' as the proverb nearly goes.

King Ignacio Did the Solemn Prince just make a joke?
And one at my expense? Falconer, lock it up and give me
the key. I've never liked that bird, it reminds me of your
dead mother.

> *Music, sinister. Falconer exits with Zephyrus, who still*
> *squawks hostilities at the King.*

The Light Princess was in your sights. A disgrace.

Digby If I'm to wear the crown, I won't be known for
killing unarmed women. You drummed your beliefs into
me, but I know my own mind and the fact is you know
nothing about Lagobel – nor what divides us.

King Ignacio (*in Digby's ear*)
> Here's a proverb for you, son:
> 'Kings have lengthy arms.'

(*To a Soldier.*) Bring me Lady Delphine.

> *Exit Soldier. Enter Falconer with a key, which she*
> *gives to King Ignacio.*

Word's arrived King Darius has rooted out a husband for that foreign witch that you kissed. I must kill them before they breed or there'll be floating babies everywhere.

Proverb: 'Children play with fire,
Children will get burned.'

Enter Soldiers flanking Lady Delphine, sixteen, miserable, frightened.

Ah, you remember your second cousin Delphine? Bride material.

As the proverb has it, son:
'Kings are gods on earth.'

Ceremony tomorrow. Llewelyn, you're best man.

Llewelyn Yes, Father.

King Ignacio
Let the bells ring!

NOT A FAIRY-TALE

Music continuous as King Darius enters with Mr Grey, Serjeant-at-Arms, Courtiers and Servants. Mr Grey tries and fails to get the word 'No' out – 'N-n-n-n-n-n' – throughout the following.

King Darius
Let the bells ring!

Lagobellans gather. Piper is pushed at aggressively; she hides somewhere.

Lagobellans
The King has had his challenge met
But we are not persuaded yet —
We'll either sing 'Hallelujah!'
Or it's the day for a coup d'état!

King Darius People of Lagobel, news to make your hearts soar! Bow to this patriot, Mr Grey. He's found in our gold a silver that when extracted and joined with pepperleaf, produces what shall be known as the Descending Nostrum – available to all light children who need a dose. Yes: he's cured our daughter!

All turn, as to the majestic 'Althea Selma Isadora D'Arcy' theme, she walks on, wearing a hoop skirt. She wears her golden crown, and carries orb and spear. They are removed. She doesn't rise. Gasps.

And having met the challenge, it's a royal wedding. Kiss her!
Let the bells ring!

Lagobellans
Let the bells, let the bells ring!
Let the bells, let the bells ring!

Piper
Tell me it's a
Fairy-tale

I am seeing?

Is
That Princess

Althea Selma Isadora

D'Arcy?

Lagobellans
Celebrate
This glorious day!

Jubila-
Té!

Jubilaté!

Let the bells sing! –

King Darius
Let the bells ring!

Lagobellans
Let the bells, let the bells ring!
Let the bells [**Men:** ring], let the bells ring! –

Piper
It must be a fairy-tale

I am see-
Ing.

King Darius
Now she can
Rule
Our Lagobel!

Keep from harm
Our
Yell-
Ow
Land!

At
Long last she's
One of us!

Lagobellans
Hallelu,
Hallelu,
Let the bells ring
Let the bells,
Princess!

Hallelu-
Jah, hallelu-
Jah,
Princess!
Let the
Bells [ring], let the bells
Ring!
Hallelu-
Jah,
Hallelujah,
Princess!

Let the bells
Ring!
Cele-

Desperately, the stammering Mr Grey tries to lift Althea's skirt, but is stopped by King Darius. Serjeant-at-Arms notices and so does Piper; her lone protest is drowned out; she is pushed violently.

Piper No! Did you see that?!

Don't believe
This
Fairy-tale!

Brate and jubilate
And
Celerate and ju-
Bilate and

King Darius *and* **Lagobellans**
Let the bells ring!

Lagobellans
Let all the bells
Let all the

King Darius *and* **Lagobellans**
Thank God! –

Dear God! –

                        She is –

This is –
A lie!   – Grounded!

All
Althea Selma Isadora
D'Ar—! D'Ar—! D'Arcy, D'Arcy!

GOD, THE HORROR

Piper creeps through gloomy palace corridors towards Althea, holding a candle, ducking and diving in the shadows.

Piper
God, the horror, my Princess.
I will search on ev'ry palace floor;
Ev'ry door! Where are you?
God, the horror, Althea . . .

NO H2O

Althea, standing in a stately room. If she walks here, her face betrays pain, though her hoop skirt hides the cause. Bells and cheers outdoors.

Piper There you are. This wing is a labyrinth.

Althea It's the Monarch's Wing. You didn't expect the heart of the kingdom to be ordinary.

Piper What's happened to you? Are you hurt?

Althea No. Don't come near me, please.

Piper But how, how?

Althea Didn't you hear Father? My husband-to-be Mr Grey.

Piper 'Extract of silver and pepperleaf' – come on!

Althea Whatever the medicine, it works.

Piper gingerly makes to caress her. At once, Althea puts out her hand: touch me not.

Piper I'm your friend. Your only friend.

Althea People like me don't need friends. I have a cheering public.

Piper All I've ever wanted is what's best for you . . .

Althea We were forced together as children, Piper, but our lives are incompatible now. Don't cry.

Piper Why wouldn't I? I don't believe you've chosen this.

Althea Yes, I have: I've always been in control of my destiny.

Piper Why do you always do this, Althea? The day you face a truth and feel and weep like a person with a heart is the day I'll believe you. I *know* something's happened –

Music, urgent.

For God's sake, what's wrong with you?

Althea
This is a moment
Like the day of my birthday
When they said, 'Mother's dead.'
Quite a
Reason to sob,
Trouble was there was a
Mob who was sobbing for me!

So I bucked up and said no to their crocodile woe.
It's the same thing,
It's a moment:
I have a choice and it's cling
To my life or I die.
I'm a princess,
So don't expect less:
My eyes are dry,
Only babes cry.
Now's the moment:
Piper, they want me,
God, I misread them!
I'm bred for this; I will wed them!
It's my fate, it's my duty.
Bring me scissors to cut off these juvenile locks:
It's the stocks if you do not obey me!

Piper Althea –

Althea
Oh, I know! the woe! the woe!
Look at me, though –
Not a tear flow,
No H2O,
My eyes are dry,
Only babes cry.

Piper And the cost to get to this glorious 'moment', or doesn't that matter?

Althea
It cost childhood,
It cost brother,
My confinement,
And the death of Mother . . .
It cost Digby
And the feeling
That he gave me –

Feeling like no other . . .
But the real cost
Was whoredom,
And torture
By my father.
But I have the stomach and heart of a king:
I'm through it and now's the moment.

Piper And if the final cost is you?

Althea
Not a tear flow,
No H2O . . .
My eyes are dry
If it's goodbye.
All this weeping,
In our desert, it's bizarre –
I'm a D'Arcy,
Heartless brutes, that's what we are.

Piper Is that really true, Althea? You'd torture people?
That's what you said. What did he do?

*Althea's childhood music. She lets Piper touch her,
then look beneath her hoop skirt. Everything is
bloody; she has been weighted, her body 'solidified' by
a medieval golden contraption bolted into her thighs,
callipers, robot-like body armour.*

Forced you? Broke you? Pinned you –?
Braced you –?
God, help you –
God, help us –
Althea!
I could cry for Lagobel,
I could weep my whole life long
Till we would be completely
Under water, for ever!

Althea Let me . . . please.

She runs a finger across Piper's cheek.

See your tears flow –
This H2O,
Does it begin to express

And she puts Piper's hands on her own heart.

This emptiness?
If the answer is yes
Then it's true, I must be heartless
I must be dead in here
Because I can't cry!

Help me as far as Mother's grave. I'll say goodbye there.
I'm leaving and this time I'm not coming back.

Piper But you can't live out in the world by yourself.

Althea You always said I could do anything. Please, dear
friend, I'll never forget you. Help me out of these
manacles, and then let me go. Then you'll never have to
cry for me again.

ZEPHYRUS CALL, ALTHEA *reprise,*
DARKEST HOUR *and* GRAVITY!
*In Sealand, Digby is trapped in military manoeuvres with
Soldiers. Sealand military drums. He sings his Zephyrus
theme against the percussion.*

Digby
Zephyrus, so
Zephyrus I
Honour my father, deny my love . . .
He has us caged,
I hear your cry –
What if I go?
What if I fly?

He breaks free of manoeuvres and the Soldiers melt away.

You are, you are Althea –
You are all of the world to me,
You are heaven-sent!
Althea, where will I find you?
Our lake?! . . .

He runs off. Althea is seen in the moonlit trees, grounded, free of contraption and skirt, stained with blood, walking slowly towards the lake. She is wearing the weight-inducing crown, and holding the golden orb and spear.

Althea
I feel light, even in my darkest hour,
The weight of this truth, it calms me.
To be light, grounded by a heavy heart
And by the deeds they have done.
Then let the night show me the way,
Will darkness complete me?
Even invite shadow to stay
As I gift the lake each silent ache
That burns endlessly.
Lovely lake, wellspring of all living things,
This paradise on earth, she calms me.
Water of life, give me my eternal sleep;
Oasis of blue, my grave.
So let the night show me the way,
Let darkness complete me;
I now invite shadow to stay
As I gift the stars my silent scars
That burn endlessly.

She reaches the water, and enters it.

I feel light, even in my darkest hour,
I feel light . . .

*The golden crown, orb and spear take her under.
Where she was in the sky, she is now in the water. She
struggles awfully. And then she is gone. Enter Digby
through the trees.*

Digby Althea? Althea?

*He exits. Althea rises with a gulp, surprised she
doesn't float into the air. The music recalls 'Levity?'.
She can swim, beautifully.*

Althea No . . . is it . . . it can't be . . . is it . . .

Gravity I am feeling?

Enter Digby.

Digby Althea!

Althea Digby? Oh, Digby, you're here . . .! Look . . .
look at me . . .

Digby Your're down here?

Althea Yes, but I'm not drowning . . . and I'm not being
forced or weighted . . . I can barely breathe, Digby . . .

Gravity! I am feeling:
It's the water,
Keeping me from rising,
Yet I have a notion
That I have more motion . . .
Gravity:
It's the lake
Holding me,
Whispering that I am safe . . .

*Digby, having entered the lake, laughs for the first
time in his life.*

Althea What? Stop laughing at me, stop – what is it?

Digby
I feel,
I feel,
I feel light!

End of Act One.

Act Two

Lagobel. King Darius. Mr Grey, in his wedding suit.

King Darius Where is she?

Drums. Lagobel's mob, with newspapers: 'Princess Missing'.

Lagobellans
He lost his son and heir and
Now he's gone and lost the spare!
The fugitive Princess! –
He said her abnormali-
Ty was absolutely cured!
A dirty royal whopper: propaganda and spin!

King Darius (*reading newspaper*)
'The King deserves the chopper' –
That's a treasonous lie!

Sealand. King Ignacio. Lady Delphine, in her wedding dress.

King Ignacio Where is he?

Sealanders, with newspapers: 'Wedding Postponed'.

Sealanders
'The King said in a statement
That the marriage has to wait –'
The fugitive Prince! –
'Because his solemn son is
On a mission in the West.'
A filthy royal heap of bleeping rubbish and spin!

King Ignacio (*reading newspaper*)
    'More power to the people' –
    This is treacherous dirt!

Lagobellans *and* **Sealanders**
    There never was a wedding,
    We were totally misled!

King Darius	**King Ignacio**
Where is she, where?!	Where is he, where!

Lagobellans *and* **Sealanders**
    A rotten royal crock of cock and bull and spin!

Sealanders
    We've nothing but disgust
    For such a shame- / less lie!

King Darius
    She's vanished in the dust,
    And left me high / and dry!

King Ignacio
    It's only wanderlust:
    He'll eat his hum- / ble pie!

Lagobellans
    How ludicrous to trust
    A harpy in the / sky!

King Darius	**King Ignacio**
This will not stand!	This will not stand!
Lagobellans	**Sealanders**
Propaganda	Propaganda
And / spin!	And / spin!
King Darius	**King Ignacio**
Where has she gone?	Where has he gone?
King Darius *and* **Lagobellans**	**King Ignacio** *and* **Sealanders**
Where has the	Where has the
Princess gone?	Pri-i-ince gone?

AMPHIBIAVA

*The lake. Rhapsodic music. It's teeming with life. Althea
and Digby swim; swans glide, dragonflies fly, lilies bloom,
frogs leap suggestively.*

Digby

  With this crown of reeds and crimson lilies,
  I name you Althea Selma Isadora D'Arcy,
  Queen of the Lake.

Althea

  With this crown of reeds and crimson lilies,
  As well as swan feathers and tadpole larva,
  And this wee teeny china-blue-green thing,
  I name you Digby Ignacio Dylan Constantine,
  King of the Lake.
  King of our Kingdom,
  Actually Queendom,
  Actually our new Democratic Republic
  That I now name –

A green frog leaps into her hands and the name is:

  – 'Amphibiava'!

Digby

  Amphibiava?

Althea and Digby

  Amphibiava!

Digby

  Here we don't fight and stain
  The water beneath our feet –

Althea

  Sweet water!

Digby

  – With blood
  As they do in those, those other places –

65

Althea

Those places –

Digby

In *this* oasis –

Althea

We merely swim
In our crimson crowns –

Digby And?

Althea And?

Digby *and* **Althea**

And fall!

Althea

Like this!

Ebullient instrumental and they 'fall' underwater together. Splash! Something goes on down there: the fecundity above tells us so: the lake and Wilderness are alive. Water plants start to fruit! Minnows hop. The lovers resurface.

Look, there's minnows, fruits galore –
A feast fit for a King, King D.

Digby

And this dragonfly is your footman –
Loyal in lake or sky, Queen A!

Althea

And this teeny china-blue-green thing
Is your royal steward, King D!

Digby

And this lily leaf is papyrus
For your great proclamations, Queen A!

Althea

From this lily-leaf papyrus,

In this safe place
I now proclaim –

Digby
She now proclaims –!

Althea (*speech to the whole lake*)
What's mine is yours!
Yours is mine!

Both
Ours is ours –

Althea
For ever!

Both
Theirs is theirs –

Digby
Yours: all mine;
Mine: yours, for ever!

Althea
For ever!

Digby
So come and join us here
In this calm oasis.

Althea
In the night's
Dim
Light
We glimmer
And swim –
And fall . . .!

Digby
The night's dim
Light –
We glimmer –

And fall . . .!

Althea
That's all!
Amphibiava!

Digby

For ever . . .

Althea

For ever . . .

Digby

Fall with me for ever . . .

Althea

For ever . . .

TINKLE, DRIZZLE, BUBBLE AND GUSH

Music, urgent. The lake remains visible in this sequence. Althea does little but swim. Digby kisses her all over. We go from day to night to day. Water lilies close with the moon and open with the sun. Swans sleep, their feathers ruffle in night's chill; they wake with dawn. Night-toads appear in the dark, then disappear at day. Something like time-lapse photography. We see King Darius, still edgy over the newspapers, and Mr Grey, still in his wedding suit, asleep. Enter a Servant and Serjeant-at-Arms.

King Darius Wake up, Mr Grey. Till she's found and you're married, we're in a state of alert.

Servant King Darius, your Serjeant-at-Arms.

King Darius Where have you been?

Serjeant-at-Arms Your Majesty, I'm beginning to question your parenting skills . . . but I think I know where your daughter is. What will you give me if I tell you?

King Darius How dare you blackmail me?

He immediately gives her his golden fob, ring, etc.

Gold, gold: now speak!

We see King Ignacio and Lady Delphine – still in her wedding dress – as a Courtier and the Falconer enter.

Courtier King Ignacio, the Falconer has news of your son.

Falconer Your Majesty, in return you must let me free Zephyrus.

King Ignacio I want you to kill Zephyrus.

He gives her a key.

Free the damned bird: now speak!

Serjeant-at-Arms	**Falconer**
There is a lake,	
	A secret lake –
It's in the Wilderness.	
	The Wilderness.
I think	
	I think
She's with him,	
	He's with her,
The Prince,	
	The Light
No	
	Prince-
Less . . .	
	-Ess . . .

At the lake.

Althea *echoed by* **Digby**
Tinkle, drizzle, bubble and gush!
Sprinkle, spatter, trickle and splash!
Tinkle, murmur, gurgle and dash!
Sprinkle, ripple, babble and rush!
Tinkle, drizzle, bubble and gush!

Music urgent. Sealand. King Ignacio; Falconer with a map; Llewelyn.

King Ignacio Llewelyn, I want you to redeem yourself for not killing her.

Llewelyn Anything, Father.

King Ignacio Bring your brother home. Fail and I'll banish you.

Llewelyn But where is he?

Lagobel. King Darius; Serjeant-at-Arms, wearing her gold, and with a map; Piper.

Servant Your Majesty –

King Darius You. The only person to whom my daughter listens. You helped her escape.

Piper I refuse to speak to you. I'm an orphan, so send me to the orphanage.

King Darius If you don't redeem yourself, I'll send you to the gallows. Go with her to Althea and persuade her to come home, whatever it takes.

Piper You know where she is? – Where?!

King Darius
A lake,

It's in
The Wilderness.

King Ignacio
A hidden lake

It's in

The Wilderness.

Piper (*to herself*)
The secret lake
That gives us life!

Llewelyn
A hidden lake?

King Darius
She's there!

King Ignacio
He's there!

Retrieve her –

Retrieve him –

Or it's

Or off

The

You

Chop!

Hop!

Dissolve Lagobel. In Sealand, Falconer, with Zephyrus, and Llewelyn prepare to leave. Zephyrus is agitated by King Ignacio, as usual. The King studies the map. Shimmering lake music.

King Ignacio Keep him away from me.

Falconer He knows the terrain better than anyone, sire.

Llewelyn Hurry –

King Ignacio Wait. You say this lake is *here*? It's not fed by a tributary from our river, is it? Could there be a headway out of it, flowing into creeks in their desert?

Falconer
The lake is here –

King Ignacio
And *here* is
Where it flows to Lagobel.

Falconer
Yes, sire –

Llewelyn
  The lake's the source that
  Waters all of Lagobel?

Falconer
  Well, yes –

King Ignacio
  So if I dam our
  River *here* the lake would dry!

Falconer
  But if you dammed our river, sire –

King Ignacio
  Then Lagobel will die!

  Oh, what a plan,   **Llewelyn**
                                 You mean?

  How sweet,
                                 You mean?

  I liquidate
                                 Annihilate?

  Them all;
                                 You mean?

  The kingdom,
  The Princess –
                                 You dry

  It's death
                                 Them

  By
                                 Out?

  Drought!

Althea
  Here within this ultramarine,
  Iridescent, emerald scene

72

Father has no say in my life,
I am safe from terror and strife;
Endless bliss, for ever serene . . .

NOTHING MORE THAN THIS

A new day. Althea, swimming. Digby away from her.

Althea Come in, take my hand.

Digby Take mine, come out.

Althea Out? You look pensive.

Digby I miss Zephyrus. And food.

Althea Look at all the food: minnows, berries, green
algae –

Digby Althea, I was thinking that I might build us a bed.

Music, jagged.

I could chop down those trees,
I could build us a house . . . over there!
Let me build us a house!

Althea
Why? You sound very stern:
Is it you're wanting to make me a dutiful wife?
To cook and darn socks?
A spouse in a house?

Digby
No, Your Majesty, no . . .
I mean a home – God, help me say this –
For the day when the stork
Brings a child.
Well, she might
Bring a child?

Althea

Child?! You sound like the King.
This is my home, it has everything, I need
Nothing more than this!

Digby

Nothing more than this?

Nothing more than this,
Nothing more than this!   Nothing more than this?

Digby

But, Your Majesty, *think*.
Winter out here grips like death –
The chill, the ice! –
There will be nothing to eat!

Althea

So? I'll sleep with the birds!
Now I suppose you will argue that birds do not
Hibernate?

Digby They don't! –
The first sign of frost, they're out of here:
It's fly or you die!
I will build us a house!

Althea

This is my home, I have everything, I want
Nothing more than this . . .

Digby

Nothing more than this?

Nothing more than this,
Nothing more than this!   Nothing more than this?

Althea Digby, look at yourself: you're all solemn again.
Don't you get the gift of this place? –

Stay in the lake,
Here you'll know
Levity for ever . . .

74

*Digby re-enters the lake, resistance ebbing. He
disappears below the surface.*

No grief or ache,
Fear or woe –
We'll stay here for ever . . .

Digby surfaces abruptly.

Digby
This change that's happened, this love we are feeling
Has confounded the fates, and now they're appealing
That we face our kingdoms and declare our love!

Althea Our kingdoms? Where I'm hated? Why are you
doing this?

Digby
This star-crossed passion, this springtime sensation,
It has shifted the ground; the fates' expectation
Is we stand together and we change the world!

Althea For God's sake, this is the world *here*, our
paradise –

Digby But why can't you leave it, even for a moment?
Come and live like a normal person. You chop the wood,
I'll darn the socks –

Althea Stop demanding things of me, Digby, you're
worse than Father. I'm not what he wants and I'm sorry
if you feel the same. I'm safe here, away from shackles.

Digby But you think you have true gravity here, yes?

Althea Yes.

Digby So prove it.

Althea You're not hearing me –

Digby
The fates are urging, the fates are imploring,
You and I are in love, the world needs restoring –

75

Althea Stop it, *stop tormenting me.* You can't hurt me here, no one can. I'm free of Father and my shining knight of a brother and Mother rising to heaven as the strangers wailed . . .

Digby Your mother? Tell me about your mother, Althea.

Althea When she died, the shadows tried to tear me down . . . but they couldn't reach me. The air didn't have shadows and nor does this place. You wouldn't understand.

Digby I lost my own mother, Althea.

Althea Oh, I know, you cried and cried like the soft and Solemn Prince that you are. There's no place for that stuff here.

Digby So it is true. You are so light you can't feel.

He gets out of the lake. Night falls.

Althea
    Amphibiava!
    Amphibiava!   **Digby**
                            Nothing more than this?

    Nothing more than this,
    Nothing more than this!   Nothing more than this?

Althea
    If you loved me you would stay . . .

Digby
    If you loved me you would leave . . .

Althea Then that's it. There must be no love between us.

Digby None. Love is something serious. And you make light of serious things.

Althea Well, I'll leave the crying to the Solemn Prince. Go. I don't love you. I want the lake, not you.

A noise above.

Digby Zephyrus?

Zephyrus arrives.

Someone's here.

He doesn't notice as Althea takes a deep breath and disappears underwater. Enter Llewelyn and Falconer from the direction of Sealand.

Llewelyn Digby. Why have you done this? Where is she?

Digby turns to see that Althea has disappeared.

Digby?

Digby She's dead.

Llewelyn You have to come back to Sealand with me. If you don't, I'm banished. (*To Falconer.*) Search for her.

Digby I killed her, she's dead.

Llewelyn Father's lost his mind – you're the only one who can placate him. I need you, come home.

Digby All right, Llewelyn. I'll do whatever Father wants. I never loved her.

Llewelyn Zephyrus! Zephyrus! (*To Falconer.*) Call him. Hurry.

He exits after Digby. Althea emerges before the Falconer exits. She goes under again. Zephyrus circles the lake. Falconer, sensing something, fills her water pouch from the lake and drinks a little. She looks about – perhaps she finds Digby's dead lily-crown.

Falconer Is she here, Zephyrus? Does he love her?

She exits after Digby and Llewelyn. Althea rises. She sees Zephyrus. Zephyrus leaves.

Althea emerges.

Althea
> For ever,
> Night after night in my lake,
> Nothing more than this!
> Beyond that shore is loss and suffering,
> Nothing but war and regret.
> And he just said that I am dead to him
> So I'm sure there's nothing more:
> Night after night in my lake.

As she sings, time passes. Night gives way to day. The sun beats down hot, too hot. The animals and birds betray anxiety. Leaves begin to curl, the world begins to change. Althea does not yet realise it, but her water is going down.

> For ever,
> Day after day in my lake,
> Nothing more than this!
> So my rapport is with amphibians?
> So I deplore Digby's ways?
> Well, he declared he never cared for me –
> And therefore there's nothing more:
> Day after day in my lake!

At last she notices. Music, insistent, anxious.

> Something's wrong.
> The inlet has stopped.
> And if the inlet's not flowing the
> Water is draining away.
> Can it be true?
> Dear God, the level is plummeting,

Look at the animals fret.
Digby's told them of Amphibiava,
Of my heaven on earth where I'm safe!
I never loved him, so now he's betrayed me!
I must hold on, I must never give up,
I must fight to stay here where I'm . . .
Light . . . light? Light . . .

As the sun beats down, the water evaporates and drains away.

I am Queen!
Queen of the Lake! –
I am Queen!
Queen of the Lake! –
I have everything, everything I need.
Nothing more than this!
I need nothing more than this!
I need nothing more than this!
I want nothing more than this!

Her head collapses like a rag-doll's. Her crown of dead lilies falls off. The last of the water drains and she rises, her dress in tatters, muddy and dripping, unconscious, water weeds trailing from her dress. Enter Piper and Serjeant-at-Arms from the direction of Lagobel.

Piper Althea! Althea!

DROUGHT

Music grooves as the lake is lost to sight. Lagobellans including Mr Flowers and Mr Crabbe, looking at maps, newspapers, etc., panicking.

Mr Flowers
So this lake –
Very queer –

Sort of acts
Like a weir –

Mr Crabbe
Do you know
Who deduced it?
The Princess, I swear.

Mr Flowers
From the East
It is fed –

Mr Crabbe
From the West
It is *bled*!

Mr Flowers
She was right –

Mr Crabbe
All our water
Flows westwards from there!

Mr Flowers *and* **Mr Crabbe**
If Sealand's aware –

Lagobellans
But they wouldn't dare!
But they would!
Holy hell!
Ev'ry tap!
Ev'ry well!
Ev'ry stream,
Ev'ry river:
Is suddenly bare!
Ev'ry creek!
Ev'ry loch!
It's the foe
Run amok!
And she warned

Of the danger –
That girl in the air!

Time passes, they become more thirsty, more desperate.

Ev'ry tide	**Mr Flowers** *and* **Mr Crabbe**
In retreat!	We
Ev'ry trough!	Are
Oh, the heat!	On
Ev'ry tank!	The
Ev'ry fountain!	Brink!

Lagobellans 1
There's water!

Lagobellans
Where, where?!

But there isn't any: it's a mirage.

There is no	**Mr Flowers** *and* **Mr Crabbe**
Water flow!	Help
We are doomed!	Us,
Oh, the woe!	We
And she warned	Must
This could happen!	Drink . . .!
She said to beware!	
There's some kind of dam!	
Is this genocide?	
We're dying of thirst.	We will die
This country is cursed.	Of thirst.
The sweltering sun.	Lagobel
A scorching abyss.	Is cursed.
What will the King do?	
This is genocide!	This is genocide!

A stately room in the Palace, with King Darius, Serjeant-at-Arms, the stammering Mr Grey, Guards. Althea is forcibly strapped to a bed, being seen to by the King's Physician and Piper.

King Darius Tell them the army's been deployed and the water will flow again soon.

Serjeant-of-Arms What army?

King Darius They must ready themselves: she weds Mr Grey tomorrow. Drought or not, I need an heir.

King's Physician Sire, she's fading fast, she must drink.

King Darius (*sotto, to Guard*) I know I have stores, you haven't looked hard enough: the cellars. (*To Serjeant-at-Arms.*) Now, I promised you and the pauper a reward.

Serjeant-at-Arms Sire, you do realise it's the drainage lake? When it's thirsty, so are we. Althea told us the day her suitors came, but we didn't listen.

Althea stirs.

Piper Althea? (*To King Darius.*) Don't touch!

King Darius I beg your pardon?

Piper I always wanted her on the ground. But not by your methods.

King Darius You may take your reward and go, we have no use for you any longer.

Piper I had to bring her home, Mr Grey. But I do know the truth.

King Darius Pauper, you know nothing. How could you?

Piper And to think when the Queen was alive he was known as the Kind King.

King Darius That's enough.

Piper Take off these straps, she's dying.

King Darius No. I won't lose her again. You're not a father, nor a king, so you could never understand. None of you could.

Piper
Because she's a girl, because she is 'light',
You think you can deny her what's right:
Decency, kindness, fairness, grace,
Not a trace –
She is your daughter!

King Darius
Daughters may be unwilling, and
Daughters kick out at the world:
When they choose the wrong thing
Then the choosing is down to the King.
One day she'll thank me –

Piper
There is blood on your hands
And you know it, sir!
It's Althea's! –
(*To others.*) I swear on my life that he tortured her!
(*To King Darius.*) And though your wife's not here
You will listen as if she were:
She'd say, 'You've lost your right to be King.'

King Darius
I am King.

Piper
Yes, Darius, King of them all!
Thank God for him
For bringing her down!
God, what a man –
He saved the crown!

83

Althea's down!
All hail the fairy-tale King!
I would never live like you . . .

And if it doesn't rain none of us *will* live – because you
didn't listen to her.

King Darius Be careful, pauper . . . this is close to
treason . . .

Piper (*re: Mr Grey*)
        Treason to say he's not to be blamed?
        Treason to say you crippled and maimed?
        Bolted her to an iron brace,
        The disgrace!
        You don't deserve children!

*Rubbing at his hands like the lady from the Scottish
play, King Darius is now losing this argument. During
this the King's Physician examines Althea more closely.
Other Servants and Guards start drifting in.*

King Darius
        Children may be ungrateful, and
        Children know naught of the world.
        When they scream, 'This is me!'
        Then it's time that they change, don't you see?
        My father changed me –

Piper
        See him rub at his hands:
        They will ne'er be clean!
        Althea's blood!
        I swear on my life I saw things obscene!
        And since his wife's not here
        Then the pauper will play the Queen
        And say, 'You have no right to be King.'

King Darius
        I am King!

Piper
Yes, Darius, King of them all!
Thank God for him
For tearing her down!
God what a man –
He saved the crown!
Man of renown! –

King Darius What evidence? You accuse the King, you need *proof*.

Piper I can see it in Mr Grey's eyes.

King Darius I am King . . . I am King . . .

I am King!
King of you all!
I am King!

He finds his Physician in his face as the music holds.

Physician Your Majesty. I'm afraid that when Princess Althea dies . . . which she will if you don't do something . . . her child will die with her.

King Darius What? I, I don't understand.

Physician The Princess is with child.

A moment. Music.

Serjeant-at-Arms
Though our land's in thrall to drought
How our tears fall –

Piper
How our tears flow –

Serjeant-at-Arms *and* **Piper** *with* **Lagobellans**
Oh, the sorrow,
Oh, the woe . . .

MY LITTLE GIRL'S SMILE

*Thirsty dying Lagobellans process past Althea offering
dying flowers, a march of sorrow. King Darius takes the
straps off Althea. She seems to levitate.*

King Darius
On one hand, if I am King,
Then I am father to the thousands –
It's them I had to choose,
To them I've paid my dues.
But I would trade, trade my crown
Right about now
Just to see my little girl, yes my little girl –
Just for a while
I am asking –
Just to see my little girl smile,
Just smile, this once for me.
On this hand, all that's left
Of my kingdom is now in pieces.
If they were in my shoes,
Then they'd have had to choose!

Serjeant-at-Arms
If we were in your shoes
Then we'd have had to choose.

King Darius
So for this land, I have been strong,
And I have fathered all of the thousands –
But *still* they fall and bruise!
I choose, yet *still* they lose!
Yes, I would trade, trade my crown –

King Darius *and* **Piper**
Right about now
Just to see –

King Darius
My little girl –

Serjeant-at-Arms *and* **Piper**
Your little girl.

King Darius
Yes, my little girl –

Serjeant-at-Arms *and* **Piper**
Your little girl.

King Darius
Just for a while, I am asking

	Serjeant-at-Arms *and* **Lagobellans**
Just to see	Just to see
My little girl –	Your little girl –

King Darius
Smile,
Just once, just this once for me
Please, let me see
My little girl –

Serjeant-at-Arms *and* **Piper**
Your little girl.

King Darius
Just smile,
This once, just this once for me, for me.

BITTER FATE

In Sealand, King Ignacio, Digby, Llewelyn and Lady
Delphine are on a balcony. Somewhere, the Falconer.
Thousands of cheering Sealanders beneath. Soldiers and
Courtiers dotted about. King Ignacio's theme ripples

King Ignacio Hear that? You must have missed it.

Digby Yes, Father.

King Ignacio Then let's tell them of your mission. (*Orates.*) Prince Digby has returned: how could you doubt him?

Cheers. His public speech continues in pantomime as Digby and Llewelyn separately voice private thoughts.

Digby
This is it, I submit –

Llewelyn
I yield –

Digby *and* **Llewelyn**
I will serve the crown no matter what.

Digby
I am the solemn prince;
And to be the solemn King's my lot.

King Ignacio . . . And you must honour him for great daring . . .

Digby *and* **Llewelyn**
Nothing ever changes
In our realm of blue.

Digby
I turn my back on all delight,
On all the joys I knew.

Digby *and* **Llewelyn**
I've no memory of my mother –

Digby
And I never knew a princess,
Wear the crown, bear the weight:

Digby *and* **Llewelyn**
This is fate . . .

King Ignacio . . . For Digby's discovered we're the masters of their water. He's overseen the building of a dam that's stopped our river from flowing into a lake that waters Lagobel.

Digby
> What was that? What a lie, what a trick –
> I am plunging into an abyss –

Llewelyn
> Controls and plots and traps –

Digby *and* **Llewelyn**
> So my life is nothing more than this?

King Ignacio ... The Princess is dead! Next, every Lagobellan, and with all resistance quashed, he'll lead the army and seize the gold.

Digby and Llewelyn
> Nothing ever changes –

Digby
> Father's grand design –

Llewelyn
> Should I have chosen banishment?

Digby
> And all his sins are mine.

Digby *and* **Llewelyn**
> Mother's faded from my memory –

Digby
> And the Princess is a phantom,
> Wear the crown, bear the weight:

Digby *and* **Llewelyn**
> This is fate,

Digby
> Bitter fate ...

King Ignacio ... And tomorrow it's a royal wedding!

Cheers, and immediately, Zephyrus's theme, lush and urgent.

ZEPHYRUS'S JOURNEY

Falconer
Zephyrus, I

Zephyrus call!

Zephyrus appears, magnificently.

Roar with the West Wind
That bears your name.

Zephyrus lands on her glove. She takes her water pouch and attaches it to the bird.

I know that you know
She makes his soul stir . . .
So fly! –

She launches him and he flies off.

Journey to Her Highness in the sky . . .

THE WEDDING

Lagobel and Sealand. In Sealand, a church is being readied for the royal wedding: red carpet, beautiful flowers. In Lagobel, where the flowers are dead, King Darius, Piper and Serjeant-at-Arms are beside the floating/levitating Althea. The King is asleep. Piper writes a letter.

Piper
'Dear Prince Digby . . .' (*To Serjeant-at-Arms.*) What do I say?

Serjeant-at-Arms
When you met her, you were be- / guiled,

Piper
'You were be- / guiled –'

Serjeant-at-Arms
She said when you saw her you / smiled.

Piper
'Saw her you / smiled –'

Serjeant-at-Arms
Now her light is flickering / out –

Piper
'Flickering / out –'

Serjeant-at-Arms
You alone can save us from / drought.

Piper
'Save us from / drought –'

Serjeant-at-Arms
You should know she's –

Serjeant-at-Arms *and* **Piper**
Carrying your child.

Piper
'Carrying your child . . .'

Serjeant-at-Arms *and* **Piper**
Carrying your child . . .

Piper – Oh, what's the point?

King Darius I don't expect forgiveness, Piper. I'll sit here in my sackcloth and ashes till I die.

Serjeant-at-Arms Sleep, sire.

Zephyrus appears, flying into Lagobel. In Sealand, the Falconer is seen in the church.

Falconer
Zephyrus, hurry, the wedding's at sunrise!

Zephyrus arrives at Althea and lands on her. Piper and King Darius are amazed.

Falconer
  Dear God, have you made it? I think so, I feel it!

Piper
  I know that bird, he belongs to the Prince!

King Darius
  Water!

  He grabs the water pouch. Piper takes Zephyrus.
  Music continues.

Piper He can carry my letter!

  That's her first concern, and she puts her letter in
  Zephyrus's beak as King Darius rushes to Althea with
  the water.

Serjeant-at-Arms Wait, sire! What if it's King Ignacio's
last cruel trick: is it safe?

King Darius I'll drink some first.

Serjeant-at-Arms But, sire –

King Darius If nothing happens to me by sunrise, I give it
to her.

Piper	**Falconer**
Yes, Zephyrus,	Yes, Zephyrus,
Take this!	
	The wedding's tomorrow but
I know that you know	I know that you know
She makes his heart fly,	She makes his heart fly . . .

  So roar, roar through the sky! –

  Zephyrus flies off. A musical interlude. A magical
  choreographed journey of the bird from Lagobel to
  Sealand, and of time passing: of King Darius, Serjeant-
  at-Arms and Piper waiting, sleeping, fidgeting; and of

the wedding scene in the church in Sealand coming to magnificent fruition: wedding guests including King Ignacio, Falconer, Bishop, et al. A bright new day, and a wedding march suddenly rings out. Digby and Llewelyn enter the church. During the following, in Lagobel, King Darius wakes and he wakes Piper and Serjeant-at-Arms.

King Ignacio Do you have the ring?

Llewelyn Yes, Father. Digby, I –

Digby There's nothing to say. I'll be King. Each day I'll do my duty; you'll do my bidding; we'll repeat, *ad infinitum.*

Lady Delphine appears in her wedding dress and processes towards Digby. Zephyrus arrives in the church. During the following, he tries to go to Digby but Digby shoos him away, so he must either drop the letter, or the Falconer is in receipt of it.

Sealanders
God save Delphine,
God save Delphine!
The future Queen!
God save Delphine!

Llewelyn has either picked up the letter or the Falconer has thrust it at him.

Llewelyn
'Dear Prince Digby . . .
She said when you saw her you smiled . . .
You should know she's carrying your . . .'

King Darius
Dear God, please, God, save my –

Llewelyn *and* **King Darius**
Child.

*King Darius gives Althea the water. Lady Delphine
reaches Digby. The Bishop opens his Bible. Althea
revives.*

Piper
God, the wonder –

King Darius
My daughter . . .

Llewelyn (*re: letter*)
Digby, read this, for God's sake!

Piper
Are you waking, or am I asleep?

Llewelyn
Do you love her?
Digby, I could weep –

Llewelyn *and* **King Darius**
Althea!

Piper
I could weep –

King Darius
My daughter . . .

Piper
God, the wonder –

Digby
Althea . . .!

Althea My lake, my lake, my
lake!

*She pours the remaining
water all over herself.*

Digby She doesn't love me,
only her lake.

Llewelyn But if it's true?

I don't understand . . .

King Darius My child, you'll never forgive me.

King Ignacio Bishop, get on with it!

Bishop Wilt thou have this woman to thy wedded wife, to live together after God's ordinance . . . (*Etc.*)

Althea Why are all the flowers dead?

King Darius Drought. You were right, your lake's the source.

Althea Sealand drained it. They must have dammed the inlet.

. . . so long as ye both shall live?

Why's no one retaliating?

King Darius We're devastated.

King Ignacio (*to Digby*) Answer!

Althea Then, Father, give me a spear.

King Darius But the drought has caused misery; the Wilderness will be more dangerous than ever.

Llewelyn I know where the dam is. We fight our way through his henchmen, demolish the wall, and the water will flow again.

Althea We have to find the dam –

King Ignacio Digby!

– there's no choice.

Llewelyn There's no choice: do you love her?

95

Suddenly, Digby runs from his wedding. Llewelyn follows. Chaos music.

King Ignacio After him! Go! Bring him back to me!

The Falconer launches Zephyrus towards the Wilderness as the scene changes.

Falconer
Go, Zephyrus, follow
Your friend and defend him,
Call all of the birds in the sky!
You know the Wilderness,
Ev'rything's crashing
So fend off his foes, they must die!

CRASH IN THE UNIVERSE

Pounding, syncopated music. The stars are out. Digby is running, over mountains, along the river towards its dam/diversion east of the Wilderness. Llewelyn follows, covering. Zephyrus flies above them. King Ignacio's dogs are set upon Digby. Sword out, he is a fearless fairy-tale knight. He surges ahead of Llewelyn, jumping walls, turning corners, slaying anything in his path.

Digby
I must fly
Through this crash
In the universe.
I must fly,
No, roar
And destroy the dam!
Fill the lake with water,
That is now my quest.
I have always loved her,
I must save her!

Soldiers give chase to the runaway Prince. Piper is

*seen pulling Althea towards the Wilderness from
Lagobel. Experienced now, they are fearless fairy-tale
warriors.*

Althea
Resolve to be the Queen now
Rises in my breast.
Fill the lake with water:
I will save her!

Digby fights off the Soldiers.

Digby
I'm the son of a bad king:
Is that a curse?

                Althea
                I'm the child of a lost king:
                Is that a curse?

No: I fly –

                No: I fly –
Through this crash –   Through this crash
In the universe.   In the universe.

*All the birds in the kingdom appear, led by Zephyrus,
swooping ahead of and after Digby and Llewelyn.
Althea, Piper and Serjeant-at-Arms arrive at the lake.*

Althea My beautiful, dying lake. Sealand did this. We
need to follow the inlet east towards the dam.

Vengeful dragons appear.

Piper Althea, watch out!

The dragons attack: they fight them off.

Althea
I'm my mother's daughter,
This is now the test –

Piper *and* **Serjeant-at-Arms** (*and* **Lagobellans**, *off*)
Her Highness is a beacon blessed –

Althea
I was born to shine –

Piper *and* **Serjeant-at-Arms**
Born to shine, born to shine –

Althea
Empress of the West!

Piper *and* **Serjeant-at-Arms**
Shine on, Althea!
Shine on, shine, Althea!
Shine on, she will shine,
She will shine, shine on! –

Althea
We must fly through this crash
In our universe.

Piper *and* **Serjeant-at-Arms**
For Althea we fly –

Althea *and* **Piper** *and* **Serjeant-at-Arms**
Through this crash
In our universe.
We're Queen material!

Althea East! To the dam!

Focus on Digby and Llewelyn, pursued by Sealand Soldiers.

Digby
Highness in the night sky:
You're a beacon blessed.
If you cannot shine,
I can never / rest.

Sealand soldiers
Sealand evermore!
Sealand evermore,

Sealand evermore,
Ever more, evermore!

Digby
I must fly

Through this crash

In the universe.
For Althea
I fly
Through this crash
In the universe.

Llewelyn
We must fly

Through this crash
In the universe.

Through this crash
In the universe.

Llewelyn The dam! Brother!

*He throws Digby a cudgel to pummel the wall that
has made the dam. He covers Digby, shooting and
slaying, as Digby climbs the wall.*

Digby
You are, you are Althea!
You are all of the world to me –

Sealand soldiers
Sealand for evermore!
Sealand for evermore!
Sealand for evermore,
You traitorous son!

Digby
You are, you are heaven-sent –
Here are your
China-blue
Fountains,
Blue fountains –

Sealand Soldiers
Sealand for evermore!
Sealand for evermore!
Sealand for evermore!
Sealand for ever / more!

Digby bashes the obstruction with brute force. With each hit it weakens.

Digby *Fall down!*

Sealand Soldiers
Sealand for ever / more!
Digby *Fall down!*

Sealand Soldiers
Sealand for ever / more!

Digby *Fall down!*

Sealand Soldiers
Sealand for ever / more!

Digby *Fall down!*

Sealand Soldiers
Sealand for ever / more!

Digby *Fall down!*

Sealand Soldiers
Sealand for ever more!

Sealand military drums. Soldiers overwhelm Llewelyn. Out of the pack emerges King Ignacio, with his gun.

Llewelyn No, Father! No!

King Ignacio shoots, Digby falls.

Digbyyyyyyyyy!

Bass drums pound an ancient-sounding rhythm as suddenly the thousands of birds attack the Soldiers. Zephyrus targets King Ignacio and tears his eyes out.

TEARS *and* GRAVITY *reprise*
The dam wall gives way. A tsunami. Digby is caught in the water, tossed and turned. Water rolls into the

Wilderness, flooding it, to strange, shimmering music.
Enter Althea with the wind, discovering her water, her
ribbon caught, horizontally, in a tree. She is windswept
but ecstatic. She sings bits of her childhood tune.

Althea

Tinkle, drizzle, bubble and gush . . .

The water settles in the lake. Eerie silence. The filled
lake is beautiful. Althea hovers above. Digby floats on
the surface of the water. In its blue-green ripples are
stripes of blood red. Zephyrus flies to him in distress.

Water, my lake . . . my lake . . . Help me down . . . Pull
me, the lake . . . Piper, where are you? Zephyrus, my
lake . . .

She laughs, ecstatic-hysterical. But she can't get down.
She is frantic at her lightness; it has never been so
disabling.

Tinkle, murmur . . .

You . . . whoever you are, my lake . . .

Zephyrus squawks at the floating body.

Zephyrus? Digby . . .? It's you? I know you're trying to
take it from me again. You won't . . . I want my lake and
I'll kill you to get it, I'm so light and unfeeling I'm
capable of it . . .

Zephyrus flaps his wings at Digby.

Digby? Digby, stop this . . . please. Because you didn't do
this, did you . . .? Digby . . .

Stay with me, darling, stay with me . . .
You look so fragile . . .
Yes, you did this . . .
Just stay with me,
Look into my eyes, my love.

You could never do me harm,
God, I know that now
Because you love with everything you are,
You give with all you have to give,
But my love for you
Has come much too late . . .
I could weep
My whole life long,
Future years
With you now gone – I'll cry
Until we both are
Underwater for ever . . .
See my tears flow?
This H2O
Is filled with regret –
Without your love
These tears don't even begin to express
This empti—

She is crying so intensely the world is silenced but for her weeping and tears plink-plunking into the lake. Enter Piper and Serjeant-at-Arms. The weight of Althea's tears brings her down. She cradles Digby in her arms, kissing him.

Digby? Digby . . .

Digby opens his eyes. Zephyrus flies again. Enter Llewelyn, exhausted, and Falconer.

Digby Tears.

Althea What?

Digby Tears. They've brought you down to me.

Althea Yes, I think they have . . . But you're hurt, your shoulder, you're bleeding.

Digby My father . . .

Althea No, I hurt you, and I'm so sorry.

Digby Althea.

Althea You're smiling. I've never seen the like, it's half blinding me.

Digby But wait, we can't stay in here, we have to get out.

Althea Just stop talking, please, don't leave me –

Piper Althea, he's right, you have to get out, the baby.

Althea What?

Digby (*to Piper*) Yes?

Piper Yes, the baby, the baby!

Althea Baby?

Piper Well, you know, with everything else on our plate, I completely forgot to tell you.

Althea Very well, then. Let's go. Let's face the world.

The Solemn Prince laughs as the Light Princess gets out of the lake and stands.

Piper Hello.

Llewelyn Hello.

Serjeant-at-Arms Hello.

Falconer Hello.

The pulsating 'Gravity/Levity' theme as Althea helps the injured Digby out of the water.

Digby
Gravity, are you feeling?

Althea
Gravity I am feeling . . .

Digby
Gravity!

Althea
I am feeling
Free of fears: drow-
Ning in the sorrows,
Fading in the shadows,
Fears no more!
Free of ropes, and
Ribbons, oh the wonder
Tears of joy I
Should've cried before!
Gravity I am feeling
Free finally . . .

Digby
Free finally . . .

Althea *and* **Digby**
Walking beside you hand in hand
Always, for the rest of our lives.

Althea
With tears in my eyes –

	Digby
I'm down	You're down
From the skies –	From the skies –

– I have found my gravity,
Gravity,
Gravity . . .

EPILOGUE: ONCE UPON A TIME,
MY FAIRY-STORY *reprise*, *and* CORONATION

Piper
Once upon a once a –

Llewelyn
    – once upon a time . . .

Piper
    lived a Princess –

Llewelyn
    – and a Prince –

Piper *and* **Llewelyn**
    – in kingdoms –

Piper
    – gold –

Llewelyn
    – and blue –

Piper *and* **Llewelyn**
    – united by a Wilderness of emerald.

Piper And so the Princess, at last allowing herself to feel loss, found her own way down, weighted by her tears. So much weight, in a thing so light.

Llewelyn The Prince, loving and at last receiving love, smiled such that his heart floated.

Piper Althea did become Queen, but most importantly she went to university and became a marine biologist. And I? – I became Lagobel's first Prime Minister.

Llewelyn And I, the Prime Minister's husband.

Piper As for the lake –

Llewelyn Fragile –

Piper Beautiful –

Llewelyn Life-giving –

Piper Both kingdoms declared it a protected place.

Llewelyn The Prince's father, a bad king, died alone, blinded by the birds. One bird, Zephyrus, who once belonged to my mother, became famous throughout the lands for his deeds.

Piper The Princess's father – a kind king who, grieving for his wife and son, had lost his kindness – lived a year longer. In the moments before he died, he told Althea that her mother would have been very proud of her, and that he was too.

Llewelyn When the time felt right, there was a simple ceremony in the old style.

Coronation music. The Wilderness.

Piper
A Coronation!

Llewelyn
First song of the Maytime –

Piper
Coro-   **Serjeant-at-Arms**
                                         A Coro-
Nation!
                                         Nation!

Llewelyn *and* **Falconer**
Echo through the land!

Piper, Llewelyn, Serjeant-at-Arms *and* **Falconer**
Ev'ryone hear it!

Everyone emerges from the gold and blue lands and converges in the green one. Someone holds the baby.

Company
Ringing out! Ringing out!
Never to cease!
Bringing us, all of us –

Sealand and Lagobel! –
Bringing us, all of us
A gift of peace,

Sealanders
For your Queendom of Gold –

Lagobellans
For your Kingdom of Blue –

Company
For the whole world!
For the whole world!

*During the following, Digby crowns Althea, then
Digby takes the baby.*

Digby
Let all the bells start pealing –

Althea
Ring on this sweet a-blossoming evening –

Digby
As through the blooms a Sealand King –

Althea
Comes to his Queen as it was intended.

Company
Let all the bells start pealing,
Ring on this sweet a-blossoming evening!

Digby
Hand proferred in peace, the Sealand King –

Althea
Joins with his Queen as it was intended.

Company
Peace in our land as it was intended!

Althea *and* **Digby**

    A Coro-

                             Company
                               Coro-

    Nation!

                               Nation!

    A Coro-

                             Company
    – Nation!
                               Coro –

    Anthem
                               Nation –
    For a new day.
    A new spring –

                               New spring –

    Dawning –

                               Dawning –

    Hear the people's voices!

Company
    Ev'ryone hear it!
    Ringing out! Ringing out!
    Song from above!
    Bringing us, all of us –
    Sealand and Lagobel! –
    Bringing us, all of us
    A gift of love,

Sealanders
    For your Queendom of Gold –

Lagobellans
    For your Kingdom of Blue –

Company
    For our nations of green!
    Emerald green for an emerald Queen!
    Emerald green for an emerald Queen
    For the whole world!

Some Ensemble	The Rest
Ringing out!	Coro-
Ringing out!	Nation!
Ringing out!	Coro-
Ringing out	Nation!

Queen Althea, King Digby, their daughter, families and countries. And they all lived reasonably happily with the occasional skirmish until they died.

The End.